Katha D. Blackwell

1

Not Another Victim

Not Another Victim: A Woman's Guide to Avoiding a Bad Relationship
Copyright © 2008 by Katha D. Blackwell

ISBN: 978-0-615-51503-8

Interior and Cover Designed by: Katha D. Blackwell
Cover Background purchased from Istockphoto.com

Katha D. Blackwell

~~~

Thanks and appreciation goes out to my husband Eric who has always encouraged me to fulfill my dreams. He has been a voice of wisdom at times when I did not know what to do. Thanks for supporting me!

And of course my greatest appreciation goes out to the Father, the Son and the Holy Spirit, who gave me the gift to write, to learn and courage to inspire others. Without You I am nothing.

~~~

Not Another Victim

NOT ANOTHER VICTIM

~~~

A Woman's Guide To Avoiding a Bad Relationship

Katha D. Blackwell, MSW

Contents

Not Another Victim

DEDICATION

This book is dedicated to my only daughter Eliana.
And
All my nieces in Georgia, Texas and Illinois
My prayer is that you all will never be in a
bad relationship.

Not Another Victim

Introduction

Dating the wrong man is like taking the wrong prescription. By the time you have swallowed it's too late to spit it out. It's already in your body. I want readers to see this book as a stomach pump. The kind of pump that will rip out every lie that has been told about relationships and release a new mindset for women.

Thousands of women across the world have been mistreated, abused or murdered at the hand of a boyfriend or husband. With so many domestic violence agencies being shutdown, there has to be a greater movement beyond the norm to prevent bad relationships.

Although many domestic violence advocates believe there is no way to avoid abuse, I believe that with careful examination and discernment women can avoid dating the wrong man. The information provided within this book in no way excuses the behavior of abusive men nor does this book blame women for getting into an abusive relationship. No one can control the actions of another person. Everyone has free will to make a decision as to whether or not they will abuse another person. So please rest assure this is not that kind of book.

Many may ask who this book is designed for? The answer is simple. If you know of someone who has been abused then this book is for you. If you do not ever want to get into a bad relationship this book is for you. If you are someone who wants to see an end to domestic violence then this book is for you. If you are a teenage girl, then this book is for you. Bottom-line, if you are a woman this book is definitely for you.

Within this book, are several chapters addressing the many questions that victims of abuse have after getting out of an abusive relationship. Many abused women find themselves in a relationship with another abusive man right after getting out of an abusive relationship.

This book is designed to equip women with the knowledge they need in order to avoid any relationship that can tear down their self-esteem, self-worth and their relationship with God. The primary focus of this book is to help women acknowledge the little things that could have taken place in order to avoid getting involved with the wrong man. The little things described in this book include the following: your relationship with God, self-esteem, forgiveness, financial independence and setting boundaries in every relationship.

It is my hope that this book will bless every reader regardless as to whether you are a woman or a man. By following the steps in this book, you will be taking steps in a direction that is free from violence.

Thank you for taking the time to read this book and if you have any questions or comments please visit my website at www.kathablackwell.com

Not Another Victim

STEP 1

Check Your Heart for Unfinished Issues

Not Another Victim

SELF-ESTEEM

A wonderful woman I had the honor of meeting shared with me some revelation about the story of Adam and Eve. As many of you know Adam and Eve lived in the Garden of Eden and one day the serpent came and enticed Eve to eat of the forbidden fruit. During their conversation, the serpent caused Eve to question who she was. In Genesis 3:5, the serpent tells Eve that if she eats of the forbidden fruit her eyes will be opened, and then she will be like God, knowing good and evil. The main thing to focus on regarding this scripture is the "be like God" part. Eve had already been made in the image and likeness of God, but the serpent caused her to question who she was. Imagine what Eve was thinking...I want to be like God. I'm not good enough, there is something missing. Eve's action is one of the main reasons why so many women have a negative self-image of themselves. We constantly question whether or not we are smart or pretty enough. In order to avoid a bad relationship, we must maintain a secure level of self-esteem. One of the most important things that everyone needs is a positive self-image. Self-esteem is the way you feel about yourself and view yourself. Another way to look at self-esteem is to look at it as the one thing that tells you although several mistakes have been made there is still a way to keep moving forward. Self-esteem is something that you are born with and is reemphasized throughout your life. I have never met a baby who thought he was fat or short. It is the environment in which people are raised that can either boost self-esteem or diminish it. Without a good self image, negative thoughts can lead you to depression and bad decisions. Whether you had a poverty stricken childhood or a very prosperous one, a healthy self-image can be established. If you do not have a secure level of self-esteem, it is encouraged that you refrain from engaging in any relationship or even date. The reason being is that you have to secure a positive view of yourself that says "I'm beautiful" regardless as to whether or not anyone else thinks so.

Many women have informed me that their ex made them feel good about themselves in the beginning. They received positive words from him that they had never received before and this is what led them to become interested in him. The compliments, the flowers, the dates, the feeling of being pursued by someone, the attention, all of these attracted them to abusive men. And although healthy relationships have these same qualities, abusive relationships stem from power and control. Without a strong level of self-esteem, your new boyfriend can turn into someone who has the most influence over your life. That influence later turns into power, which can later turn into control.

The main thing to understand is that no one should make you feel better than you make yourself feel. Even if you are in a healthy relationship it is your responsibility to build your self-esteem. It is important that you build this area of your life before you start dating. In an abusive relationship, the abuser fulfills a need initially. The need to be loved, the need to be provided for, the need for companionship, whatever the need is the abuser usually fulfills that need. And if you are lacking a secure and strong level of self-esteem you could fall for the wrong man. Any man can start off as a smooth talker, a motivator or a friend to confide in and later become a nightmare, but for a woman who has low self-esteem he will appear to be a dream come true.

As a child, my sister and I were fat. We were literally F-A-T. In today's medical terminology we would have been diagnosed as obese. Our clothes were definitely coming from the Misses department, surely you have gotten the full idea of what I am trying to say. However, in the midst of all that fat our father would constantly boost our self-esteem. One thing my father always did was tell us that we were beautiful. He reemphasized our beauty so much that eventually it became engraved in us, and we believed him. As I grew into my teenage years, I was not impressed when a boy would call me cute. I knew I was cute because my father had already laid that foundation, and I agreed with that foundation. If you were not raised in a self-esteem building environment, there is still hope for you to undue the negative words that have been planted into your heart. This is the simplest thing you can do... speak positive words to yourself. This is a very important part of any healthy relationship and an excellent way to build your self-esteem

A Secure Level of Self-esteem

How often do our actions depend upon the actions of another? A secure level of self-esteem encourages people to do things alone without needing a companion. For example, going to the movies independently is something that many people avoid because they have no one to go with them. Having a secure level of self-esteem means that regardless as to whether people like you or not, you like you. You believe in you. You believe you are capable of starting your own business. You believe that although things have been rough there is an opportunity for a new start. A woman with a secure level of self-esteem can say to herself..."I can make it regardless as to what my life may look like." Before getting into another relationship this is what you should be able to say to yourself.

Despite all the things that have happened in the past it is so important for you to be your number one fan. In Romans 12:3, the word of God directs us not to think of ourselves more highly than we ought to. This is implying that you should think greatly of yourself, just not to the point that you think you are God or take advantage of God's mercy. Rather you should think of yourself as being someone who is precious and important. A person who has been made in the image and likeness of God. Wow! We all have been made in His image, and that is something that should be highly thought of.

So before we move on to the next part of step one let's rate your level of self-esteem. Please allow the following questions to assist in determining your level of self-esteem:

Number 1: Are you unable to provide for yourself and your children(if applicable)? Even if you are not you should be establishing a plan to become financially stable. Lacking the money to provide for your family can greatly impact anyone's self-esteem. Take the necessary steps to address these things. We will discuss employment in another chapter.

Number 2: Is there something physically you would like to change about your appearance? And are you able to change it? For instance, you cannot change your race...if you are black you are black. If you are latin...you are latin. If you are white...you are white. You cannot change that. Is there something else you would like to change? If you see yourself as being extremely fat or too skinny, or have some acne problems or whatever it may be, figure out a way to address these concerns. Feeling good about your appearance does a lot for a person as well as builds your self-esteem.

Number 3: Are there some things in your past that

you regret and have difficulty forgiving yourself about or difficulty forgiving someone else? Forgive yourself and the other person. The one thing that can choke your self-esteem completely is by holding a grudge against yourself. Everyone in this whole world has done something that they wish they hadn't done. What makes your situation hold more weight? Let it go. It happened and you can't go back and change it. What you can do, however, is learn from the mistake and grow from it. This is what you have learned not to do. With every bad decision comes a greater level of wisdom. Use that wisdom to help you grow. Do not choke the growth that can take place and help you in making better decisions.

Maybe the shoe is on the other foot, and someone has wronged you in the past. Perhaps you were molested as a child, or raped, or abandoned or cheated on, whatever it is, do not accept it as being okay, nevertheless, forgive the person not the act that was done. Forgiveness does not mean reconciliation or friendship. What it means is a greater level of freedom for yourself.

We will further discuss the power of forgiveness in another chapter. Forgiveness alone is powerful and deserves it's own chapter. So for the sake of self-esteem we will table forgiveness for a later chapter.

<u>Number 4:</u> Do you have a hard time thinking of something nice to say about yourself? One thing victims of abuse have difficulty doing is saying something positive about themselves. If you have something constructive to say about yourself then say it. And I am not talking about a New Year's resolution. I am talking about something you see or feel. For example, maybe you have great eyes or a brilliant smile, or maybe you are one of the best cooks in your family. Maybe you are an excellent mom or a good friend. Whatever it is you should start to say that more often.

If you answered "Yes" to any of the questions, there is a strong possibility that your self-esteem is not at its highest potential. And getting into any intimate relationship right now would not be beneficial to you.

If you are already in a relationship, there is a good chance that it is not as healthy as it could be and now would be a good time to put the relationship on hold. I am aware that this may be hard for some of you, yet I encourage you to find a way to build your self-esteem outside of this relationship. I prefer that you take a break from the relationship that you are in so you can focus on yourself. However, for those of you who are married, I suggest you take some time for yourself each day. It doesn't have to be a lot of time just some time to encourage yourself. Take some time each day to focus on yourself. During this time you should begin to speak out those things you want to achieve in your life. For instance, if you want to be successful, you should say, "I will be successful." If you want to be debt free, you should say, "I will be debt free." There is power in the words that you speak so take that hour to build your self-esteem by speaking against ever negative thought that discourages you. Additionally, during this hour start to write out some plans for how you can achieve the things you desire. For example, becoming debt free will entail viewing your credit report.

Building your self-esteem starts with speaking more positive things about yourself. You have to be the driving force behind building yourself up. If you answered "No" to any of those questions, then you have accomplished part 1 of step 1 towards avoiding a bad relationship.

WORDS
OF
FAITH

(Say these words to yourself)

"I am beautiful. I am strong. I am smart. I am fearfully and wonderfully made in the image and likeness of God. God has personally designed me in a unique way that is priceless. Right now, I am ignoring every negative thought that tries to tell me that I am not good enough, smart enough or pretty enough. Today, I am making the decision to build myself up with my words and actions. At this moment, I will no longer entertain negative words that have been spoken to me from other people. Today, I confess that my self-esteem is up and not down. It is in the right place that it should be. From this day forth, I will never speak another negative word about myself nor will I allow other people to speak bad about me."

Katha D. Blackwell

John 1:12 (NIV)
Yet to all who received him, to those who believed
in his name, he gave the right to become children
of God

John 15:5 (NIV)
I am the vine; you are the branches. If a man
remains in me and I in him, he will bear much
fruit; apart from me you can do nothing.

Ephesians 1:5-6 (NIV)
He predestined us to be adopted as his sons
through Jesus Christ, in accordance with his
pleasure and will— to the praise of his glorious
grace, which he has freely given us in the One he
loves.

Romans 8:37 (NIV)
No, in all these things we are more than
conquerors through him who loved us.

Not Another Victim

HEALING

If you want to move on with your life, it is essential that you heal from the past hurts. Many of us go through life carrying past hurts and burdens that old situations left behind. I call these old situations baggage. Although you do not see the baggage you are carrying you may be able to feel the weight. Just like luggage can eventually become heavy after carrying them for awhile, so can hurt feelings and broken hearts. Maybe your health is not good or maybe your blood pressure easily rises at the slightest situation. These are signs that healing needs to take place. Just take a minute and think about all the horrible things you have been through. Think about the people who hurt you. Before you keep reading this book take some time and really think about it. How do you feel after thinking about what happened to you? Are you angry? Mad? Sad? Or are you at peace? It's amazing how something that happened so long ago can still impact your emotions today. You may not want to remember the pain that you went through. It may be too much for you to bear, but every wound needs to heal. And just like a physical wound all bandages must come off in order to heal. God has come to heal us from everything that tries to keep us in bondage, and if you are living with a broken heart, anger, unforgiveness, or sadness he can heal that too.

Everyone in this world at some point in time or another has had to deal with being hurt or disappointed. Whether your heart was broken because of an abuse, rape, drugs, alcohol or bad decisions, God can heal you. How long will you allow past issues and mistakes to affect your heart? How long will those issues control your life?

Unfinished issues and hurt emotions can control your life. How do they control your life? By hindering you from loving someone else, by influencing your every decision, by putting up walls with everyone you come in contact with due to lack of trust. Please do not act like everything is well with you. Everything that has been pushed under the rug needs to come out! If you avoid certain topics because they are similar to what you have been through, there is some unfinished business in your heart.

One goal that every woman should keep as a priority is to heal from every abusive relationship. Time is the one thing that is needed in order to heal. Just like any wound with time you will heal. However, if you do not give yourself time to heal you will do more damage to yourself and slow down the healing process. Our society is such a rush rush nation. In order to fully heal you need time. For example, if you broke your arm playing basketball, it would not be wise for you to go and play basketball the next day with a broken arm... why? Because there is a strong chance that you will make your injury worse. The same thing goes for a heart that needs healing. It is not wise to get into another relationship after just getting out of one.

If the previous relationship meant anything to you, why on earth would you be so quick to get into another one? This can be a huge problem and actually shows that there are some underlying issues that need to be addressed. I know this is repetitive, but it is important that you truly understand everything that I am saying.

If you are still questioning whether or not you need to heal from a past hurt let's check to make sure that you are not carrying any unnecessary baggage.

As women, we have a tendency to carry old ideas, old thoughts and old ways into a new relationship causing the new relationship to turn into the old one. For example, if your previous partner was a cheater, a liar or an abuser, do not put every man into this category. Do not assume that your new partner will be just like the old one. The new boyfriend had nothing to do with what the previous boyfriend did and should not have to pay for actions that do not belong to him. All men are not abusers. All men are not cheaters. All men are not liars. You know at least one man that is a good man...right? If you do not, let me be the first to tell you that all men are not alike. So what makes you put good men into the same category as every other trifling man...unfinished issues also known as baggage. You are carrying around bags that you were never meant to carry.

I never understood how anyone could easily break up with one boyfriend and then immediately get into another relationship with someone else the next day. This is more than just being on the rebound. You do not like being alone. And the sad part about this is getting into another relationship only covers the current hurts you have. Try being alone for at least a month and see how this affects you. Can you be single for a month or two? How about a year? Getting into another relationship quickly is just a pacifier that comforts you only for the meanwhile. Give up the pacifier. With God in your life, your heart will eventually heal, and you will gradually let go of that brand new un-forgiveness bag, that distrust bag, that hatred bag, that angry bag. How many bags are you carrying and what is inside of them? Is it worth revisiting? Yes. Especially, if you want a healthy relationship. It is dangerous to carry all this baggage and get into another relationship.

Healthy relationships consist of healthy people, not just physically but spiritually and emotionally healthy. Many women I have met have told me they never had a healthy relationship. They have had one abusive relationship after another and cannot identify what a healthy relationship looks like. I have not obtained the full understanding as to how women continuously find themselves with one abusive man after the next. Hurting women are more likely to become victims of abuse if their hurting hearts are not mended and fixed. And the only person that can fully heal your heart is the Lord Jesus Christ.

You may have tried various things in the past to feel better or to fix the problem, but truth be told all you did was put a band aide on a bullet wound. If you want to be healed from all past hurts and emotions, you must spend time revisiting the pain, praying and reading the word of God and expect God to heal you. For some of you, it may be hard to admit that you still carry around pain from your divorce, breakup, abuse, child molestation, rape or sin. However, if you need to be honest with anyone it should be yourself. What good is it to desire the greater things in life, but never be ready to receive those things or not be able to recognize good when it comes your way. Be healed today.

Every time you wake up there is another opportunity to live a healed life, a life of deliverance, restoration and peace. If you want to give up the baggage and want a new start, then I encourage you to let go of every situation that came to steal your joy, innocence, peace, trust and self-esteem. The word of God says in Matthew 11:28-30 NIV:

"Come to Me, all you who labor and are heavy laden, and I will give you rest. Take My yoke upon you and learn from Me, for I am gentle and lowly in heart, and you will find rest for your souls. For My yoke is easy and My burden is light."

Let's break certain words of this scripture down. The word laden means burdened. So he is talking to those who are heavy burdened. What I want you to focus on is the laden part. So if you are heavy burdened you need to go to God.

Go and exchange your heavy burden for His light burden. The word yoke is talking about the kind of yoke you would see on horses or oxen that are plowing a field. He is figuratively speaking of the work of the ministry. Lastly, in the last scripture He says his yoke (His work) is easy and His burden is light. So the point of this scripture is encouraging us to exchange our heavy burdens for the easy work and light burdens of the Lord. Additionally, He is promising rest. He did not say all you who are perfect come to me or all you who are sinless. No, He is talking to anyone who is carrying a heavy burden. He wants you to come to Him with all your baggage.

Your life may not have been easy, but I can tell you from first hand experience that you need strength from God to continue on with your life and have a new beginning. The Lord is desiring for you to come to Him. You are not equipped to carry all those bags so give them up to the Lord and allow Him to carry them for you. He desires for you to be healed and set free. Will you come to Him today? Tomorrow is not promised.

If you are ready to give all those past hurts to the Lord, here are a few things you can do to confirm that you believe the Lord is able to take that pain away:

#1: Open your mouth and speak (Prov. 18:21)

There is power in your mouth so you must start to speak the words in which you believe. For instance, confess that you are free from child molestation, free from that rape, free from all those abuses. Say it if you mean it!

#2 Pray to the Lord

Talk to the Heavenly Father about how you feel and expect to hear back from Him. There is no point in calling someone if you do not believe they will answer the phone. So it is essential that when you do pray expect God to speak back and by all means when you pray open up your mouth and talk. Although God knows everything, He gave you a mouth so you can speak those things that be not as though they were. Even God had to open His mouth and speak when it came to forming the earth. Follow His example.

#3 Join or Reconnect to a local church

Becoming an active member of a loving church is one of the greatest ways to stay encouraged. Find a church that you feel comfortable being a member of and continuously go there to be around other women of God. Hang out with other women of God and expect to be strengthened by the women you surround yourself with. You should be encouraged and empowered when you are around this group of women. If you're not being empowered then find another group.

#4 Renew Your Mind

The word of God says, "I beseech you. Therefore, brethren, by the mercies of God, that ye present your bodies a living sacrifice, holy, acceptable unto God, which is your reasonable service. And be not conformed to this world: but be ye transformed by the renewing of your mind, that ye may prove what is that good, and acceptable, and perfect, will of God."(Rom. 12:1-2 KJV) The word beseech means to beg eagerly. So the writer of the book of Romans is begging the reader to sacrifice your life daily to God. No longer living in sin or operating the way the world operates, but setting yourself apart. The only way you can start doing things the way God wants you to is by changing the way you think about life. And in order to change the way you think you must daily read and study the word of God. You must renew your mind. There is no way on earth for you to remain free from the past hurts and pains, unless you change the way you think about your life, your emotions, your future and the different situations that come your way. Everyday is a new day of miracles, blessings, potential stress and troubles. And with the word of God in your life you will have the strength to receive and overcome anything that comes your way. I am not saying you will not have any hard times, rather I am telling you that with God's help and strength you will make it through.

After reading through this chapter, I hope you have taken the time to evaluate your emotions and determine whether or not you are truly ready to take the next step. With continual reading and a teachable heart, you will be on your way to a greater life and better relationships.

WORDS
OF
FAITH

"By the stripes of Jesus Christ, I am healed today! I am healed from every ounce of pain, hurt, resentment, bitterness, and anger that has come into my heart. Today, I acknowledge that God is the great physician that is able to heal every broken piece in my heart. Today peace is being restored back into my heart. I lay down every emotional bag that has weighed me down at the feet of Jesus, and I have the faith and I believe that my heart is being renewed."

Not Another Victim

1 Peter 2:24 (NIV)

He himself bore our sins in his body on the tree, so that we might die to sins and live for righteousness; by his wounds, you have been healed.

Psalm 107:20 (NIV)

He sent his word, and healed them, and delivered them from their destructions.

Jeremiah 17:14 (KJV)

Heal me, O LORD, and I shall be healed; save me, and I shall be saved: for thou art my praise.

James 5:16 (NIV)

Therefore confess your sins to each other and pray for each other so that you may be healed. The prayer of a righteous person is powerful and effective.

Not Another Victim

FORGIVENESS

During several individual and group sessions, the main issue that continued to come up with abused women was forgiveness. Un-forgiveness is a dangerous weapon that has the potential of killing a true life of freedom. The bible tells us to forgive others in Matthew 6:14. And if the Lord continuously repeats Himself telling us to forgive others then we need to make sure we are applying this word to our life. This is a very powerful action that can breath life into every area of your life that needs healing. It all depends on which road you choose to take. You can either walk in forgiveness or walk in un-forgiveness. There are three areas of your life that should be evaluated in regards to un-forgiveness: Your childhood, the abuser, and yourself.

What is un-forgiveness? Un-forgiveness is the act of holding someone's faults, actions, bad decisions or mistakes against them.

Let's start with your childhood. Think back to the various situations you went through as a child. One thing that is very common for victims of abuse is being sexually abused as a child. Now why are the two of these areas connected at all? The answer is still a mystery to me. However, three out of five women that I have spoken to revealed that they were sexually molested during their childhood. Some women have never shared this information with family members and have never even brought it up until that one day in counseling. Buried burdens that have been carried throughout their life. Still painful to discuss after all those years. Sexual abuse is traumatic and has dangerous consequences on the mind of any child. And if not addressed in some form or another can be repeated throughout that child's life and come in the shape of domestic violence. This is through my own observation.

Domestic violence and child molestation are in the same category. Both are abusive and are usually committed by an intimate partner, friend or relative. Although your childhood may be hard to revisit, one of the goals of this book is to encourage women to overcome every hurt and pain. In order to truly remove these past abuses you must confront them and no longer allow them to be buried in your heart. Please do not stop reading now. You are closer than you have ever been to being set free from your past hurts and pains. If this area of your life has never been addressed or acknowledged, now is the time to address it.

Before we go any further, take the time to write down everything that you remember from the abuse of your childhood. Take either your journal or a spare piece of paper. Write down the day it happened, what was said and what he or she did to you. You can also tell someone. Just make sure the person you tell has the heart to listen to what you have been through. Everyone is not able to listen to real stories of abuse and may shut you down before you tell them everything. So for the safety of your own mind and emotions be careful in who you decide to share this information with.

If you need to cry then cry, if you need to scream then scream, do whatever you need to do, but do not allow the actions of someone else have another hold on your heart for another day. Today you are acknowledging the hurt and pain of that little girl. Maybe no one listened to her or believed her, but on today you believe her, and you are listening and you will encourage her.

It does not matter whether or not people believe you or whether you are supported right now, the fact that remains is you have to let go of what happened to you and forgive the person that committed the act against you. Forgiveness is not saying that what someone has done is okay. Sexual molestation is illegal and a vile, gross and disgusting act and is never acceptable. Your goal is to forgive the person not the act. This in no way means that they should be let back in to your life. By all means NO! When we forgive others, we are doing it for ourselves not so they can feel better about themselves. On top of that you do not even have to tell this person that you have forgiven them, unless you have the need to do so, but a simple release in your heart towards the resentment and forgiveness towards the individual is enough.

As a child, I was physically abused on several occasions by my mother's ex-husband. There were times that I went to school with scratches and bruises, yet no one really asked me what took place and my mother continuously took his side. At that time I was so filled with rage and anger not only towards him, but towards the person that was supposed to protect me...my mother. Over the years, I learned that forgiving someone is the strongest way to take authority back over your life and that is when I forgave him. I remember seeing him years later in church one day and without my heart skipping a beat I was able to make eye contact with him and say hello. My blood pressure did not raise, I was not scared, angry or intimidated. I was at absolute peace. Additionally, I learned to also forgive my mother.

When I look back over the various abusive situations that took place, I believe that she knew how crazy this man was yet was trying to figure out a way to get rid of him without him killing all of us in the process. So, what seemed ridiculously irresponsible on her part actually made perfect sense to me as I grew older. And in time I grew to forgive her and since then our relationship has become stronger than ever before. After a decade of abuse, I was finally healed walking in absolute peace. No more nightmares, no more anxiety, just peace.

All those things that went on in your childhood have to be forgiven and let go. Situations like these bring on paranoia that all men are alike. But that is not true. So if you have had any abusive situations throughout your childhood, now is the time to uncover them, confront them and address them. If you are not addressing it then how are you coping with it?

Everyone in this world has a way of coping with every situation that comes their way. How are you coping with this burden that you have carried for all these years? Are you drinking? Are you eating? Are you smoking? Are you abusing others? Are you living in fear? Are you overly sexual? Are you over eating? Are you easily aggressive versus assertive? Maybe you exercise excessively to escape the past memories that come to haunt you? Everyone has a coping mechanism, what is yours? Is your coping mechanism killing you or empowering you? Either way, now is the time to be free from those horrible childhood memories and move forward to a life of freedom. Do not let the sins of others control you for another day. This is a new day, a new season and you deserve to walk in perfect peace.

<u>Forgiving The Abuser</u>

When I discuss this part of forgiveness most of the women I have spoken to ask me how they are supposed to forgive the man who abused them and almost killed them. Additionally, they do not want anything to do with him. Let me say again, forgiveness does not mean reconciliation. You do not have to return to that relationship nor do you have to engage in any kind of conversation with him. Many women confuse forgiveness with making a mend with the relationship, and that is not the purpose of forgiving the abuser. As stated in the first section of this chapter, forgiveness is there to benefit you not the abuser. How can forgiving him benefit you? By setting you free from any kind of anger, resentment or hatred you have towards him. Anger can lead to high blood pressure, tumors, ulcers, etc. Think about every time you have ever gotten upset. Your heart rate increases and your temperature changes in response to your emotions. He does not even have to be in the room when this takes place. All you have to do is start thinking about him and all the things he has done to you. And your body automatically responds by the hurt you still have. You may find yourself needing a cigarette on the mere mention of his name. The abuse that you encountered still has some sort of control over you. If you have not forgiven him as of yet he still has control over you, one way or another. How can this be? Every person that you date gets compared to the abuser. On the other hand, you may do certain things in spite of the abuser. For example, you don't allow people to talk to you some any kind of way because of the abuser. Or you easily get upset when someone tells you what to do. These are just a few examples of unfinished business you are holding in your heart. Forgiving the abuser will help you let go of everything that has happened. It can be difficult to put your guard down after being in an abusive relationship. In order to move on and recover from all that hurt, forgiveness has to be in the picture. You must forgive him in order to be completely free from him.

It is not fair for the abuser to go on living his life, while you are still having to deal with the emotional baggage he left behind. If anyone should be living the good life, it should be you. Living well in the natural is not as fulfilling as living a peaceful life in your heart.

Forgiving Yourself

Out of all of these categories this one appears to be the hardest one for women to overcome, especially if children were involved in the abuse. For starters, acknowledge that you made some mistakes. With this area, it is necessary for you to cry out the regret that you have and the pain you feel towards every bad decisions. You cannot go back and change the decisions you made. However, what you can do is live for today and let go of the past. Even as a child, there were things I could have done differently. That pain followed me throughout my adulthood. Only until I acknowledged the guilt was I truly able to forgive myself. We all learn from our mistakes, but holding a grudge against yourself is like putting yourself in prison and locking the door. Constantly ridiculing yourself over what you should have did. The un-forgiveness you have towards yourself can become abusive. Forever reminding you of what you failed to do. Continuously putting you down, never lifting you up that is what un-forgiveness does. It puts you in another abusive relationship with yourself. So by all means...forgive yourself. Your children may have been greatly impacted by your actions. After apologizing to them, forgive yourself. Despite whether or not they forgive you the goal is to be set free from the bondage of un-forgiveness and the only person who holds the key to set you free is you.

God forgives us everyday for our actions and the one thing he doesn't do is bring up our mistakes and throw them in our face. What more should we expect from ourselves? If the Almighty God can forgive you, shouldn't you forgive yourself? No one knows what really happened but you. Be honest with yourself. Do not cover up your mistakes another day. Be true to yourself. Be true to your children and move forward with your life.

In all three of these categories the point is clear. In order to protect yourself from stepping into another abusive relationship you must be set free from un-forgiveness. This will help you become more aware of boundaries in your relationships and will also help you have a clear mind and a clear conscience.

WORDS
OF
FAITH

"Today is a new day and I confess and believe that forgiveness is in my heart. I forgive everyone that has ever abused me, mistreated me, and I especially forgive myself. Today, I am letting go of past abuses and acknowledging that God is on my side. I declare that from this day forward I am going to learn how to forgive people the way the Lord wants me to forgive people. Today, the peace of God is giving me the power to let go of every situation that came to tear me down. Today, I am free from un-forgiveness and I walk in a greater level of maturity in Christ."

Ephesians 4:32 (NIV)

Be kind and compassionate to one another, forgiving each other, just as in Christ God forgave you.

1 John 1:9 (NIV)

If we confess our sins, he is faithful and just and will forgive us our sins and purify us from all unrighteousness.

Romans 8:1-2 (NIV)

Therefore, there is now no condemnation for those who are in Christ Jesus, because through Christ Jesus the law of the Spirit of life set me free from the law of sin and death.

Not Another Victim

CHAPTER FEAR FOUR

The one thing that can lead you back to being another victim of abuse is fear. I define fear as a false emotion that fills you with anxiety, stress and dread that is influenced by past situations and the anticipation for the worst. It also constantly reminds you of the inabilities you have and the possibilities of failure. It belittles the gifts God gave and tells you that you are not good enough. Fear is a real emotion that everyone deals with one way or another. It will either be the deciding factor in your life or will be the one thing you try to avoid. Take a moment to think about all the things you do now out of fear. You carry mace in your purse because of fear. You won't date anyone who reminds you of your abuser. You have probably said or thought one or more of the following statements: "I'm scared that I will always be alone, I'm scared that I won't be able to provide for me and my children, I'm scared that I won't be able to pay my bills, I'm scared that my children will not have a father figure in their life, I'm scared, I'm scared, I'm scared.." That feeling of fear did not come from God (2 Timothy 1:7) If you are scared you are not alone. There are several women in this world that feel the same way. And maybe you have not said it out loud, but the reality of it is that everyone has felt or will feel the way you feel right now.

No one wants to live in a constant state of fear. Constantly on edge about something yet never overcoming it. The sad thing about this whole thing is that you do not have to live in fear. If you have been in an abusive relationship, you know what fear feels like. It feels like you do not have control over bad things happening to you and that is a horrible feeling. Today, I encourage you to no longer allow fear to rule your life.

The word of God says that God has not given us a spirit of fear, but of power, love and a sound mind. So if your emotions are contrary to walking in power, love and a sound mind then rest assure those emotions did not come from God.

And the only way to overcome fear is to pray, change the way you think and say. God has given us the ability to open up our mouth and pray. Pray for our families, pray for ourselves, etc. What would be the point of praying if there was no change that came along with it. God never tells us to do things that are fruitless. In other words, He would not tell us to pray for our nation, leaders and families just because it is the right thing to do. When you pray you are changing the situation around. No matter how long it takes for you to see change, you must believe that change is taking place. Everything does not change overnight so do not stop praying because you do not see instant change. Our prayers are not microwaves and may not produce what we want in five minutes or less. Yet our prayers do bring results in due season. Just like a farmer who plants his crops during seed time, he still has to wait for the crops to grow and thrive. It will be weeks or months before he even sees the budding of the seeds come out of the ground, yet although he cannot see the entire crop he knows that things are changing and growing. This is the same kind of expectation you should have with your prayers. In due time, you will see the fruit of your prayers coming into view.

What produces fear?

The motivation behind fear is a lack of

trust, a lack of trust in yourself and a lack of trust in God. With a lack of trust in our heart it is hard to believe that God will fulfill His part in our life. The Lord has made several promises to us such as being our provider, comforter and friend. These are just a few, yet with those few some of us have a hard time believing what He has promised. So instead of allowing God to fulfill what He has promised we take matters into our own hands and become our own personal God. This may sound harsh, but it is true. Anytime we solely depend on ourselves to make things happen we become our own genie in a bottle. The issue that arises with this is that without God we make several bad decisions out of fear.

One woman told me how she only stayed with the abuser because she was scared that she could not take care of herself. Another woman told me that the only reason she moved her boyfriend in with her was because she was afraid she could not pay her bills by herself. There are numerous other examples I could give, however the point I am making is that you should check the motivation behind what you are doing.

Fear should not be the deciding factor in your relationship. It should not be that due to fear you hook-up with a man who is not worth your time. Allowing fear to rule in your life will keep you away from things, opportunities and people that you should have in your life. And isn't it about time that you were able to experience the good things in life? A peaceful home, a stress free relationship and a loving family.

Here are a few steps to help you change the way you think and live a fearless life:

#1 Be Honest with yourself

If you are going to lie to anybody, please do not lie to yourself. Acknowledge the fear that you have regardless as to what you are fearful of. The first step to change is admitting that there is a problem.

#2 Walk in Peace

Never make a quick decision out of fear. In Colossians 3:15, we are directed to let the peace of God rule and direct our path. Every decision you make should be lead by the peace of God. If you read the bible you will notice that the women of God walked in peace not in fear. So when you are making big decisions that can greatly impact your life, you need to walk towards decisions that give you peace. Every decision may not be a logical decision according to our society, but as you strengthen your relationship with God, you will easily be able to distinguish between a good decision versus a bad decision. Push aside what everyone else is saying and listen to what God is telling you to do.

#3 Pray, Pray, Pray

Every man or situation that comes into your life is not a blessing. Some people and things that come into your life are filled with drama and can be a distraction. The only way you can clearly know what is a blessing and what is drama is by praying to God. Like any loving father, God does not want us to be in a situation that leads us to destruction. That is why the Bible lists several things we should not participate in or do because they are harmful to our bodies as well as our soul. No matter what your relationship with God was like in the past, recognize that today is a new day and He definitely cares about you.

Out of everything we have discussed in this chapter on fear, remember that walking in fear is not the lifestyle that represents God or the love He has for you. Living in fear will keep you in a bondage mindset and will influence the decisions you make. Today take a greater step to trust God with not just some of the situations you face, but all of them. And be prepared if things don't go the way you would prefer. Every parent has to tell their child no sometimes. You should expect God to say no sometimes as well. God truly cares about what you care about(1 Peter 5:7)so just trust that he's got your best interest in mind.

Katha D. Blackwell

WORDS
OF
FAITH

"I confess and believe that God has not given me the spirit of fear, but a spirit of power, love and a sound mind. Today, I no longer make decisions based off of fear. My decisions are made through Godly wisdom and the peace of God. Fear no longer controls my thoughts, actions or relationships. I am free from fear, I resist fearful thoughts and recognize that God is my protector, my comforter and my help in times of trouble. I am no longer afraid of being lonely or single, yet I trust that the Lord will connect me to relationships that represent Him. Today, I walk by faith and not by fear."

2 Timothy 1:7 (KJV)

For God hath not given us the spirit of fear; but of power, and of love, and of a sound mind.

Proverbs 3:25 (NIV)

Have no fear of sudden disaster or of the ruin that overtakes the wicked,

1 John 4:18 (NIV)

There is no fear in love. But perfect love drives out fear,because fear has to do with punishment. The one who fears is not made perfect in love.

Not Another Victim

STEP 2

Make Wise Decisions For Your Future

BONDAGE vs. FREEDOM

When leaving an abusive or bad relationship, regardless as to whether the abuser is cordial or volatile, it is important to make wise decisions. Every decision you make will affect your future as well as the future of your children. Emotional decisions can lead to disappointment. Do not be too quick to start doing a lot of things you haven't done in a long time. This is not the time to go on that shopping spree that you eagerly desired. Now is the time to refocus yourself and find ways to move forward with your life. If you have been in an abusive relationship for years, it is important that you take baby steps towards your independence.

You do not want to be a foolish freshman who eventually gets sent back home because they flunked all of their courses. You must get reacquainted with the old you. The person you were before the abuse and the person you have become. This is a great opportunity to reflect on where you want to go and what you want to accomplish from this point on.

When women come out of an abusive relationship, some may go from one extreme to the next...I call this the Slippery Slope of Bondage.

After women get out of an abusive relationship, they start on a new journey towards freedom. A level of freedom that entails peace, joy and excitement. And that is what a life without an abusive man looks like. The main thing for you to keep is a wise head on your shoulders. This journey can go either two ways. #1 You can either gradually enjoy the journey by making small steps towards a new level of independence. Or #2 you can quickly fast-forward to absolute freedom. The wise woman would gradually make small steps, whereas the foolish woman would fast-forward to freedom. For example, Mary Q. got out of a deeply abusive relationship along with her children. After she obtained an order of protection she immediately started acting like a freshman in college and started making foolish decisions for herself and her children. She started staying out all night, started getting certain parts of her body pierced, started to neglect her children, etc.

Another example of bad decisions is Candace S. She decided to get a divorce from her abuser. The abuse between the two of them was mutual. Her husband had decided to relocate back to his family in a completely different state and told her that she could keep the house, which was paid for, and instead she decided to go from shelter to shelter and put the house on the market. Do not get me wrong many victims of abuse want to rid themselves of every memory of abuse, but ultimately the person who has to start from scratch is the victim. And starting from scratch takes money and a lot of time. So if you are up for the challenge then go right ahead and give it all up. In my opinion, these are clear examples of what not to do. The only reason I said that is because of the many women, who struggle to get back on their feet after leaving an abuser. Now don't get me wrong I understand that an abusive relationship is like being enslaved and the taste of freedom can bring a lot out of a person, yet the decisions that follow, once you have tasted freedom, should be wise decisions.

Just think about it for one minute. Being in an abusive relationship is similar to being a slave. Master would always terrorize you and took freedom from you and now that you are free you are not accustomed to making your own decisions. Use wisdom. Do not go out into society doing foolish things. This is your life and you only have one, so instead of acting like a child with no parental guidance, be the parent, be the adult and think before you act. Put your emotions to the side for the counseling sessions and be slow to make those big decisions that will affect your life. Think about how long it took you to leave the first relationship. This may be different for some of you, but for the majority think about the pros and cons you had to think about before leaving your abuser. Where will I go? What about the children? What about school? What about money? Praise God you are free! However, every decision should be examined by pros and cons. What are the positive things that can happen from doing this and what are the negative things? Be true to yourself.

At this current crossroad, it is essential to have people, who care about you, help make some of those big decisions. It is easier to pinpoint the problems of an issue looking from the outside-in, rather than being in the situation and trying to figure things out.

People that are not in the relationship have a broader view of what is going on. That is why it is important to seek wisdom from someone that knows you and is willing to give some honest

Katha D. Blackwell

feedback of what they see in regards to what you should do. If your mother has things to say to you about your situation, now is the time to listen as long as she is encouraging you. People that care about you are not going to tell you something to harm you. They have been placed in your life to help you. Family members who criticize you or continuously point out your mistakes are not the ones who you should be talking to. If you do not have any supporting family, then seek a domestic violence counselor or even call a domestic violence hotline and talk it over. You can easily call a domestic violence hotline and share the scenario of your situation for free.

Just in case you do not have someone to talk to, I have taken it upon myself to list a few foolish decisions you should not take while enjoying this new life of freedom.

#1 Do Not Stop Paying Your Bills
Another example of foolish actions is not paying your bills in order to hurt him. For instance, if you left your car behind because he was driving it and now you decide to not pay the car payment the only person that will ultimately be affected by this decision is you. That is your credit not his. Even if it does end up with a boot on it. If the car loan is in your name, the car is your responsibility. If there are any utilities in your

71

name you need to have them turned off rather than not pay them. Who are you trying to hurt? If you have an outstanding balance on a utility bill, like heat or electricity, you will not be able to turn these items on in your name in your new apartment until these bills are paid. Praise God you left that relationship, but please do not forget that as an adult you have responsibilities that you need to take care of.

#2 Do Not Start Dating Someone Else.

This is just a bad idea altogether. You need some time to get your life together. Fulfilling your loneliness right now is not fair to yourself or the person you are trying to date while you are on the rebound. Even if this is the man that helped you leave your abuser, do not date him right now. You do not owe anyone anything so do not start dating your knight in shining armor all because he fulfilled his civic duty as a human being. Besides, I have heard countless stories from women who say that the man who helped her get out of the relationship eventually became abusive as well.

The primary goal of this chapter is to encourage you to carefully make wise decisions. The excitement that comes along with being free from an abusive relationship can direct you to do foolish things. Every decision you make from now on can drastically effect how successful leaving your abuser can be. So be wise and avoid hasty decisions.

WORDS
OF
FAITH

"Today I am making wise and Godly decisions regarding my future. I ignore foolish and quick decisions and welcome wisdom. I will not act like a child and make decisions out of my emotions. I will sit down and think about every decision that comes my way. I trust that God will lead and guide me towards the right answer when there appears to be no answer. I trust God and believe that every answer He gives me is for my good and the good of my family."

James 1:5 (NIV)
If any of you lacks wisdom, he should ask God, who gives generously to all without finding fault, and it will be given to him.

Proverbs 10:23 (NIV)
A fool finds pleasure in evil conduct, but a man of understanding delights in wisdom.

Proverbs 17:24 (NIV)
A discerning man keeps wisdom in view, but a fool's eyes wander to the ends of the earth.

Proverbs 8:11 (NIV)
...wisdom is more precious than rubies, and nothing you desire can compare...

Not Another Victim

HOUSING

There is nothing more exciting than having your own place. A place that you can call your own without the threat of being put out after an argument. A common theme of abuse that started to appear later in my counseling career was that abusers were kicking victims out. Instead of the victim kicking the abuser out it was the other way around. Literally kicking the victim and the children out of the home. Bertha M.'s live-in boyfriend of five years told her that he did not want her anymore and he directed her to pack up her things and get out. The interesting thing is that she was not ready to leave him. After years of abuse, she was being put out of his home. As if she had done something wrong to be evicted from his home, this man had the audacity to put her out. Before the victim gets fed up with the abuse, the abuser puts the victim out because he is tired of her. It should never get to that point.

With any situation having to do with mortgages and leases, there is always someone who has more authority than the other, unless both names are on the lease or deed. In most cases, there is only one primary owner/tenant, in which case a victim could easily be put out unless she fights to stay and in most cases if her life is being threatened she is less likely to fight. Getting put out could happen either way regardless as to whether your name is on the legal document or not. The goal is to make sure that you win in the end of this and if that means having your name on the document then by all means make that happen. The goal is to protect yourself from being put into this kind of situation.

Below I have listed several ways in which to decrease the possibility of you being placed into a situation as the one I described above:

Number 1: Do Not Move In with Him

This is never a good choice. If you find yourself having no home of your own and things are getting rough for you, do not move in with your boyfriend or significant other. Please do not fool yourself into thinking this is okay. If you are already homeless, moving in with him will only make matters worse. Even if he is the sweetest guy you have ever met and has never laid a hand on you...it does not matter! It is better for you to live with a relative or in a women's shelter for a while in order to get your situation in order rather than shack-up with him. If family or friends are not available then find a local shelter and go there. I have met many women who had no place to go and moved in with their boyfriend. Once the abuse started they returned back to the same situation they started with. No where to go and no one to turn to. Do not prolong the unbearable situation you may be in. You need your own place.

Even if you are engaged or planning on getting married, there is still a time and a place for everything and moving in with this man before marrying him is not the way. I know this is a hard pill to swallow, but in the long run you will agree with me. It is best to wait. Every good man is worth waiting for and so are you. It is better for you to have your own place and a sense of stability. Moving in with someone is never a good idea until you are married. Think about it this way, if you move in with him, he can always put you and your children out. Do not start to think negatively towards this situation. I truly believe that God is well able to help you. The word of God says that God is able to do exceedingly, abundantly beyond what we may ask or think. So trust in Him. You can provide for yourself and your children you just have to find a way without using a man to get there. God is able, now is the time to trust in Him.

Number 2: Find Your Own Place

Having your own home is one of the most responsible and best thing you can do. You might be unemployed and unable to take care of yourself. And if that is true it is best that you stay with a family member until you obtain adequate employment that can fulfill that need. If you are a woman that is employed it is time to find your own place. You do not necessarily have to purchase a house at this time, an apartment is a good start towards home ownership. For example start looking for an apartment within the newspaper, internet, etc. The one thing you should do is figure out whether or not your credit can hinder you from obtaining your own place. If you know you have bad credit, first attempt to repair the debt that you owe and settle the accounts. Landlords get concerned when it appears that a tenant has a problem with being faithful in paying their bills, however do not let your past credit problems discourage you from trying to find an apartment. There is a landlord out there that is willing to accept you as a tenant just keep looking.

While you are looking for an apartment, be realistic with yourself regarding the amount of rent you can afford. The last thing you want to do is sign a lease on an apartment you cannot afford finding yourself homeless again months later. Calculate your finances, listing your current bills and your monthly income then subtract your monthly bills from your monthly income. This will help you in determining whether or not you have enough money to afford a monthly rent bill. If everything calculates out well then go for it. If you need assistance in obtaining your first month's rent or security deposit contact your local domestic violence agency and try to obtain referrals for rental assistance. After you have signed the lease to your apartment, etc. put your utility bills on a budget plan.

A budget plan can be setup with both the gas company and the electric company. In the state of Illinois, we are able to put our bills on a budget plan so this may be different for your state. I personally put the utility bills of my household on a budget plan so there are no surprises with the bills. This helps me maintain a regular financial state within my household. In order to setup a budget plan, simply contact the utility company and find out what your budget plan bill will be monthly. Once you have your own place it is good to obtain a security system for your apartment. There are cheap security systems for apartments that you can purchase at most household item stores. This will just help reduce any anxiety you may have with living alone. Once you get settled into your apartment it would be good to get connected to a housing program that assists you in purchasing your own home.

One program I recommend is called NACA. NACA stands for the National Assistance Corporation of America. You can visit their website at www.naca.com. NACA is an organization that helps people obtain home ownership. I have seen them assist single women and single mothers obtain their very own property. I highly recommend you contact them in your local area and attend their seminars.

Number 3: Do Not Move Him In

This is one of the main areas that can trip women up. Although your man may not have his own place or recently got into a financial dilemma...DO NOT MOVE HIM IN. He needs to be self-sustaining. Some women may disagree, but even if he is a great man and has done many favors for you do not move him in. When you move people in with you there is no way to determine when they will move out. You are not his mother. And if he has not been able to provide for himself up until now there is a good chance that he will never be able to provide for himself and surely not for you or the family.

As women we have a natural desire to help people. It's not unusual for you to want to help him, but I encourage you to resist. The worst thing any woman can do is allow an abuser to move into her home. Even if he is not an abuser do not move him in. Once he has moved in it will be very hard to move him out. I know what you may be thinking, "It's my place so if he starts to act up I can put him out." Well guess what?...You're wrong.

The abuser characteristic is controlling. It needs to be allowed in and once it is allowed in, you will have to fight to get it out. Save yourself the drama. This is universal for every man, whether he is abusive or not. Even if he is not abusive, even if he is the best man you have ever met still do not let this man move in with you. Besides, he can always come visit. There is no need for him to move in. You should be enjoying your home alone for awhile and when the season comes for marriage then you can have another set of thighs in your bed, but for right now leave that man wherever he is. It is not your job to save him. I am not trying to be mean, yet your situation is the priority right now. You will be better equipped to help him once things are in order in your life.

Do not get me wrong, if he is in need of a place to stay you should help him, but that does not mean you should help him by allowing him stay in your home. Nothing motivates a man more than being homeless.

Just think about this for a moment, if his family won't even let him move in then why in the world should you? His family has known him longer than you have and probably know him even better than you. This is something to definitely think about. Additionally, there are homeless shelters for men. He can go stay there and if he has a problem with that remind him that this relationship has boundaries.

As stated throughout this entire book, every healthy relationship has boundaries. When my mother met her abuser he was a starving musician living out of his car. And with the kind heart that she had she moved him right on in trying to help him and he became an absolute nightmare on Elm St. And when it was time to get rid of him it was very difficult to get him out of the house and out of her life. This kind of man will not leave without a fight.

Bottom-line...whether it be an apartment, condo or house, seek out a way to find your own home. Enjoy being by yourself for a while. Decorating your home the way you want to. Enjoying life without the influence or direction of anyone else but God. Life is short and tomorrow is not promised to anyone. Isn't it worth having another day of peace and comfort knowing that when it is all said and done you have the final word regarding your home. Just imagine what it will be like to have something that you did on your own. Not because your boyfriend co-signed the lease or the mortgage, but because you did it by yourself.

WORDS
OF
FAITH

"I recognize that God has established a home for me. I believe that as I follow after the things of God, He will lead and guide me to my next home. I believe that God shall supply all of my need and will give me wisdom on how to manage my own home. I declare favor over my life with every landlord, realtor, mortgage company and bank. Today, I believe that I have all the financial need required to pay first month's rent/security deposit, the down payment and closing costs. I confess and believe that I will never miss a payment on my rent or my mortgage. There is divine order in my home and this home will represent the loving relationship I have with God. From this day forward, I am making steps towards owning my own property and being the lender and not the borrower.

Philippians 4:19 (KJV)

But my God shall supply all your need according to his riches in glory by Christ Jesus.

Matthew 7:7 (NIV)

Ask and it will be given to you; seek and you will find; knock and the door will be opened to you.

Not Another Victim

MONEY

In order to have a promising financial future, it is important that you use your money wisely. One of the main issues many women struggle with, is being able to manage their money. Not knowing how to manage your money can lead you back where you started if precautions are not taken. If you are a woman of God, your main priority is to give your tithes and offerings to your home church. Years ago, as a case manager for homeless women and children, I had the opportunity to meet several women and visit their homes. While I was visiting their homes we would go over their monthly budget. The budget would show how much the monthly income and expenses were for their household. Every detail of their expenses were written down. Everything from the gas bill to sanitary napkins. While writing down their budget I would ask them if they gave money to their local faith based institution, etc. The women who told me "No" were by far struggling more than the women who were giving regularly. Can you imagine that? Homeless women residing in a transitional housing program still took the time to give money. Barely having anything they still gave honor to God who gave them the little they did have.

These women are the prime example of faithfulness and obedience. Managing your own finances can be a challenge. Yet, if you are willing to do things God's way you will prosper. As a child of God the rules for our lives are different from those that are not saved. Not tithing causes a curse on your household. The word of God in Malachi 3:8-10 tells you the benefits of tithing and what happens when you do not tithe. 10% of all your increase should go to God. In other words, if you receive $1.00 you should give the Lord 10 cents. Every time you receive some increase whether it is from a government check or from a friend, 10% is to be given to the Lord. This sounds like such a simple task yet there are many women who struggle with paying their tithes and offerings. On the other hand there are women I know who don't tithe, but appear to not be struggling whatsoever. Do not compare your situation to there's. God gives mercy to whom He wants to give mercy to, just like a parent showing mercy to a rebellious child. So just because it appears as though they have it better, doesn't mean that their way is right. Do what's right according to the word of God and expect change.

One reason some women struggle with paying their tithes and offerings is because there is a lack of trust in God. They do not trust that God will provide for their financial needs. If the lights and gas bill need to be paid and you only have enough for those bills, it is a stretch of faith to tithe and believe that those bills will be paid. Giving your money to God out of obedience is a step of faith. If you are not giving your tithes and offerings, find out why. Do not say you can't afford to give your tithes because that is not true. In all actuality you cannot afford to not pay your tithes and offerings. God has given us His word as a guide to lead us through the life we live. There are blessings in being obedient and power in trusting God with your money. One thing I know about God is that He will never tell you to do something that is impossible. He does not lie or send you off on some lost unmapped journey. There is a reason for everything that He tells us to do. With that said, I encourage you to take a step in the right direction and pay your tithes and offerings. Your financial struggle cannot get any worse than it already has so you do not have anything to lose.

Another important action you should take with your money is stick to a budget. Many people struggle with their money not because they are not giving, but because they make foolish decisions with their money. The goal is to become a good steward over the little money you do have. God's word is true when He said He shall supply all our need (Philippians 4:19). We are the ones who spend beyond our budget and then have the audacity to be upset with God when we don't have enough money to pay the bills. For example, my husband and I make more than enough money to take care of the financial need of our household. However, due to ignorant decisions made by us, we need even more money to correct the bad financial decisions we made such as going out of state for college and having several credit cards that we did not need. This was foolishness on our end.

Buying things that you cannot afford is not living the life, it's living a lie. God has already done what He said He would do. Try not to act like He is some dead beat dad who is behind on child support payments. The less debt you have the more your money becomes available for you to fulfill the needs and wants of your family.

If I have not said enough to convince you, think about women you know that have been in a bad relationship. How were they with the money they had? Did they have enough? Did they seek out a man to pay their bills? This is not the kind of situation you want to be in. Your ability to balance your checkbook and remain within your budget will help you get to greater heights of stability. And the main goal here is to make sure that if nothing else goes right in your life you can at least say that you know how to handle your money.

If you do not have the skills with managing your money, I encourage you to find a local money management program or borrow a money management book from your local library. You would be amazed as to how much information is out there to help you.

Lastly, the main thing you should always remember is that it's not how much money you have that makes a difference, it's what you do with the little that you do have.

If you want more money continue to find ways to develop businesses or money making ideas and by all means give. Never settle for where you are financially, especially if you have dreams of obtaining more things.

Let us recap the main points of this chapter:

#1 Always Give. This should be done with every bit of financial increase you receive. Everyone who is financially prosperous more than likely gives. Whether it is to a church or to a charity giving is the ultimate way to receive wealth in return. In other words...you reap what you sow.

#2 Budget the money that you have. Staying within your budget will make a huge difference later. Here is what I stick to now, if you can't pay cash then you don't need it.

#3 Always aim for promotions and increase. You get out what you put in. How can anyone expect to receive a promotion when they don't arrive on time to work, leave early and never complete any work. Show good work ethics and be consistent. In time things will get better.

Katha D. Blackwell

WORDS
OF
FAITH

"Today I have more than enough money to accomplish my goals. I declare that from now on I will walk in wisdom regarding the money God has blessed me with. I will be a good steward over my money and purchase those things I can afford. Today, I am obedient to God in giving on a continuous basis and I trust that every seed I sow will bring a harvest to not only my house, but also to the kingdom of God. I will not go any further into debt in order to live outside of my means, however I trust that God will give me favor with the desires of my heart. I expect to see discounts and reductions on things I wish to purchase. I welcome and receive all financial wisdom that teaches me how to be a good steward over the money God has given me."

Luke 6:38 (KJV)
Give, and it shall be given unto you; good measure, pressed down, and shaken together, and running over, shall men give into your bosom. For with the same measure that ye mete withal it shall be measured to you again.

Proverbs 22:3 (NIV)
A prudent man sees danger and takes refuge, but the simple keep going and suffer for it.

Proverbs 24:3-4 (NIV)
By wisdom a house is built, and through understanding it is established; through knowledge its rooms are filled with rare and beautiful treasures.

Katha D. Blackwell

Not Another Victim

EMPLOYMENT

The one thing I always tell stay-at-home moms is that they should have another form of income coming into their home that they provide. At the moment, I am only employed on an on-call basis due to the recent birth of my son. I love my son dearly, but as soon as he turns one, I plan to actively contribute a regular income towards our family. Not necessarily by putting my son in daycare, but by finding a way that this is a win-win situation where my son can be cared for in the evening by his father. Everyone's situation is not the same, however it is highly important that you do not get comfortable staying at home with your children.

Everyone who knows me knows that I believe mothers, who are able to, should stay home with their children, but set a limit to that. The reason for my belief is that too many things happen to children who are not at home with their mother. This is one of the biggest challenges I have seen among single mothers. Which is another reason why I push so much for single women to refrain from sex. Birth control is not 100%, so it is best to keep yourself until marriage. At least then there is a greater possibility that your spouse will be around to fulfill the necessary duties of a husband, if he knows his role.

Regardless as to whether or not you are married I encourage you to obtain employment, go back to school or start a business. Whether your income comes from doing hair, freelancing, providing home childcare services, etc. it is important that you obtain and maintain some form of financial support for yourself. Part-time or full-time, just keep your hand in some sort of legal money-making activity.

One thing that is common among victims of abuse is that the abuser told the victim that he wanted to "take care" of her and that she did not have to work. This sounds good and it really is good, however he can still take care of her while she maintains employment for herself. It is refreshing and empowering to be able to have your own money. Money that you worked for. So if you decide to go to work you should do it and your husband or boyfriend should be supportive of that decision. Do not get caught up in this stay-at-home with the children mentality. If your spouse decides to leave you tomorrow, what will you do? I am not trying to discourage you from trusting men, however what I am saying is that you have to think realistically about your life. In a perfect world, where all husbands are faithful, trustworthy and reliable, I would not even suggest you get a job unless you truly want to work. But due to the fact that there are husbands in this world who either cheat, lie or are unreliable, I must encourage you to secure your own future. If he were to die tomorrow is there any life insurance available for you to be financially stable? If he were to leave you tomorrow, how would you provide for yourself? These are questions you should be asking if you are unemployed.

The main point of this chapter is to encourage you to always strive for ways to improve your career. In other words, always reach higher for promotions, for better jobs, better time slots, better pay or start your own business. Always go for greater ways of living. It is good for you to have your certification as a nursing assistant, yet it would be even better for you to become an RN.

Once you get a job in fast food go towards becoming the manager of that establishment or rather find out what it takes for you to obtain your own franchise. This way of thinking is hard for people that do not believe they can get there. If you have a hard time believing that you can have your own business or obtain a greater level of finances, I encourage you to change your way of thinking. What better way of moving forward with your life than to obtain a great level of financial income that allows you to take care of yourself without feeling the pressure of needing a man.

Money can be one of the many reasons why victims stay in abusive relationships. It is difficult to leave the financial security of someone that has provided for you for years. And stepping out by yourself can be a scary thing if the proper connections are not in place. For those of you who have been in an abusive relationship, you know how difficult it is to maintain employment if the abuser is the kind of man that does not want you to work. Or if your abuser does not work however controls the finances of the home, then again it is necessary to figure out a way to rid yourself of this man...he is no good.

Numerous women across the world solely depend on financial contribution of their husbands. The issue with this is that once he has died or left the relationship, the wife has to find a way to fulfill the financial needs of the family. This chapter is in no way trying to put anxiety on you, yet I am trying to get you to understand that unless you are financially supporting yourself, you are not in a secure position. Take a moment and think of the women you know who have found themselves penniless after a horrible break-up or divorce.

In order for you to do the best that you can to avoid becoming another victim, you must improve your financial income and become self-sufficient. If you are ready to change your situation around, here are a few steps you should take:

#1 Develop a Resume and Cover Letter

One of the most important things you should have is a resume. The first impression that a future employer has of you comes directly from your resume. You would be amazed as to how many women have either an outdated resume or do not have a resume at all. If you do not have a resume, I encourage you to connect with a friend or relative that can assist you in developing your resume. If you do have a resume, it is important that your resume is up to date and accurate. Even if you have a resume if it is over 10 years old I guarantee it is outdated. Do some research of resumes on the internet. There are several websites that show examples of resumes.

Additionally, a good cover letter, along with your resume, will show your ability to describe yourself and will also help in making sure that your resume gets to the correct person.

#2 Improve Your Computer Skills

Due to the fact that computers are everywhere, you can easily improve your computer skills. Whether you are emailing your resume or searching for a job it is essential for you to know your way around a computer. One way you can improve your computer skills is by going to the Help section of whatever computer program you are trying to learn and take the basic tutorial. Another way of improving your computer skills is by taking free typing tests online. Just do a search for "Typing Test" on the internet and several typing tests will appear. Look for the free one and take a couple tests to improve your typing speed. In one week you can go from typing 25 words per minute to 55 words per minute. It is worth increasing this skill.

#3 Improve Your Interview Skills

Once your resume lands you an interview, you need to prepare for the interview. There are several ways you can do this. First, you can go on the internet and do a search for interview questions. More than likely you will find several questions that an interviewer has the potential of asking you. Second, it is recommended that you have a mock interview with a friend or family member. A mock interview is a practice interview that will help you prepare for the real thing. It is amazing how many things people do that can hinder them from having a successful interview. Having someone interview you and give you feedback on how you did will help improve your chances of getting the job.

#4 Interview Clothing and Appearance

Once your interview is scheduled, it is encouraged that you find some interview clothes. The first impression they have of you will be the last so do your best to look your best. The main thing you should keep in mind is that this is an interview. This is not a date, a party or a family gathering. For an interview it is encouraged that you obtain a nice grey or black suit. Slacks or a knee-length skirt would be appropriate and a button down shirt. Everyone does not know how to dress for an interview so I do not want to assume all the readers are on the same page. Nothing should be revealing. If you have been blessed with various assets, please cover them up for the interview. If you have several tattoos, do your best to cover these up as well. Do not wear too much perfume, you never know who may be allergic to it. Additionally, they should not smell you a mile away before you enter the room. Last but not least, your hair should be done in a simple, yet elegant style.

Remember this key point...before you ever open your mouth in an interview, your appearance tells so much about who you are. How many times have you prejudged someone because of what they wore? Well, the same thing goes for the people who will interview you. They are already assessing your character by your appearance. So make sure your appearance is saying the right thing.

#5 Thank You Letters

After you have completed the interview, one way to keep your name on the interviewer's mind is by sending a thank you letter. Some people do not do this yet it is a common thing that is very rewarding. If there are over 50 people applying for the same job, the only way you will be able to stick out is by being memorable. Sending a thank you letter will help the interviewer remember you. A letter or a postcard is beneficial. There are sample thank you letters on the internet as well, just do a simple search as you did for the resumes.

All of these steps will help you in obtaining employment. And if you are a believer in God, please remember that the only man you need in your life is Jesus Christ. He will help you provide and can open doors for your life to change, you must first take steps towards Him.

For those of you who are already employed, I encourage you to realistically write down a household budget for your family. What is the overall cost of your bills? And how much money do you independently bring in? If you are receiving government assistance, do not include this with your budget. Government assistance could change at any time, so it is important that you figure out how much money you need to earn in order to provide for your family. There is no need to get discouraged about your financial status. God is well able to make a way for you to provide for your family. He has already told us that He won't leave us (Deuteronomy 31:8) and will supply all our needs (Philippians 4:19),so stand on the word of God and stay encouraged.

One of the hardest things victims have to do is trust that God is on their side and that leaving the abuser was the right thing to do. It's hard changing the way you think after living that way for years, yet as you constantly make a daily decision to do things God's way things slowly start to get easier. Keep moving forward with your life and expect, expect, expect to see change for the better to come your way.

WORDS
OF
FAITH

"I believe that there is a divine purpose for my life. I believe that God has designed the right job and business for me so that I may increase my current financial income. As I seek after the direction God has for my life, I expect favor with every employer, manager, supervisor and secretary I come in contact with. The favor of God is on every resume I send out and every interview I go on. I believe that nothing is too hard for God, so as I go forward in seeking a greater career move or business the hand of God is upon my life. As I walk in the direction that the Lord wants me to go, I declare that I will be patient and wait upon the Lord's plan for me."

Ecclesiastes 2:24-25 (NIV)
A man can do nothing better than to eat and drink and find satisfaction in his work. This too, I see, is from the hand of God, for without him, who can eat or find enjoyment?

Proverbs 12:14 (NIV)
From the fruit of his lips a man is filled with good things as surely as the work of his hands rewards him.

1 John 5:14-15 (NIV)
This is the confidence we have in approaching God: that if we ask anything according to his will, he hears us. And if we know that he hears us—whatever we ask—we know that we have what we asked of him.

EDUCATION

CHAPTER NINE

The most important decision you can ever make for yourself and your children is to get an education. One of the major struggles women have in moving on with their life is that they lack adequate education. I met a woman who had not obtained a high school diploma. After several bad decisions and a long abusive relationship, time pasted her by and although she had planned on going back to school she never did. And now that she has left the abuser she is looking for a job, yet every employer wants her to have a high school diploma. Look how time quickly passed her by.

Who knows why she did not get her high school diploma. Maybe she voluntarily dropped out or maybe she got pregnant at a time where teen pregnancy was unaccommodated. Either way she has an obstacle to overcome that could have been overcome a long time ago. I never found out all the details of her story, yet I had the opportunity to see her struggle with going to GED classes and trying to get a simple piece of paper so she could obtain employment. What a trial it was to watch a grown woman have to learn basic Algebra, Reading, Science, etc. This may not be an issue for you, but what about college? How long have you been trying to finish getting an Associates degree or your bachelors or your beautician's license?

An education is one of the most essential qualities a woman should have outside of a healthy relationship. Not only will you show that you can be self-sufficient, but you will also be an example to your family and friends. In order to move forward with your life you must obtain an adequate education that can assist you in being competitive with other people that are applying for the same job. It does not matter which school you go to...just GO! If you are not too passionate about going to school, then at least go and attend some training classes or a few certifications that can help you get your foot in the door. Even God with all his wonderful works has informed us that,

"Faith without works is dead"(James 2:20-26). In other words, while you are praying for God to open a door towards your future it is important that you start taking action towards your goals.

You may have a million excuses as to why you have not taken the steps to go to school. Excuses burn up your time and before you know it you will be 70-years-old still trying to get over an obstacle that started when you were 16. Today, is the day to take steps towards your future and change things for the better. I encourage you to push past the obstacles you see. If it is a financial obstacle push past that by finding the resources within your community that can help you in achieving your dream. To help you get started towards completing your education there is an organization called Women's Independence Scholarship Program that provides financial support for abused women who are attending school either part-time or full-time. For more information about this program visit their website at www.Wispinc.com. This program not only helps victims of abuse, but also helps domestic violence counselors that are in need of financial support for school.

Programs such as the one mentioned are everywhere throughout various communities. Just get connected with the local domestic violence agency or women's program within your area. Or better yet do some research online for yourself. You would be amazed as to how many programs are available for women who have been victims of abuse. Contact the local community college and find out if they have any programs for women that have not worked in a while. They may have free training programs available. If you are in a small-town by all means do not give up your search just because one person tells you no. There is a way to get through this just keep looking.

If I have not convinced you yet let me close this chapter by pointing out a very important fact. In Hosea 4:6, the word of God says,"My people are destroyed due to lack of knowledge..." That knowledge entails the understanding that nothing is too hard for God. You may have obstacles in your way, you may owe money to the last school you went to or maybe you may simply dislike a certain subject...like Math. There may be many reasons as to why you cannot go back to school, but I believe that no matter what the obstacle is, God can make a way. All you need to do is began to exercise the measure of faith He gave you and do not doubt.

Katha D. Blackwell

WORDS
OF
FAITH

"I believe that it is not too late for me to finish school. Today, I will take steps towards finishing my educational goals. Today, I will not be intimidated by what other people have accomplished, rather I will be encouraged by the many possibilities. I will not allow financial costs discourage me from completing what I have started. I have put no limits on God therefore I believe He will make a way for me to finish school regardless as to whether or not it is the school I want to go to. By finishing school, I am setting an example and influencing a way of life for my family. From this day forward, I am moving closer and closer to completing my degree and no matter how long it takes I will finish. There is nothing too hard for God."

Philippians 4:13 (NIV)
I can do everything through him who gives me strength.

Mark 10:27 (NIV)
Jesus looked at them and said, "With man this is impossible, but not with God; all things are possible with God."

James 1:5-7 (NIV)
If any of you lacks wisdom, you should ask God who gives generously to all without finding fault, and it will be given to you. But when you ask, you must believe and not doubt, because the one who doubts is like a wave of the sea, blown and tossed by the wind. Those who doubt should not think they will receive anything from the Lord; they are double-minded and unstable in all their ways.

Katha D. Blackwell

Not Another Victim

STEP 3

Set Boundaries in Your Relationships

Not Another Victim

BOUNDARIES

Every healthy relationship has boundaries. What are boundaries? Boundaries are limitations and standards within a relationship. For example, you may have set a standard in your relationship that there will be no sexual activity or that there will be no arguing in front of the children, etc. Many abused women speak about how they did not see their boyfriend or husband as abusive in the beginning, but after asking them several questions in regards to name-calling, verbal abuse, pushing, etc. it was found that the abuser was abusive from the beginning. The victim just did not see the signs of abuse due to her level of tolerance regarding his behavior. How can an abuser be abusive from the beginning and the victim not be able to recognize the abuse? The abuse is only recognized after her boundary is crossed. Everyone's boundary is not the same although it should be. Her boundary may be physical abuse, for another it may be abuse towards the children, for another it may be using weapons. For example, some victims may not leave an abuser until he threatens to kill her. He can beat her, sexually abuse her, verbally abuse her, but once he threatens to kill her that is her boundary level that has been crossed. Although this sounds ridiculous in regards to the abuse she has endured, it is very real in several abusive relationships I have come across.

Everyone has a boundary of abuse. Some have a higher tolerance of abuse than others. Check out this tolerance grid regarding the various stages of abuse:

Tolerance Grid:

Name Calling	Insulting	Intimidating	Pushing	Slapping	Punching	Threatening w/ a weapon	Child Abuse

All of the categories on this grid are abusive. Yet some people may quit the relationship after the name calling or wait until the children are abused. This Tolerance Grid can very well be rearranged in a different way, yet everything is abuse. I met a woman who knew her abuser was sexually molesting her daughter. Even though child services got involved, she actually thought about returning to him. Although this boundary was crossed she still had a level of tolerance that went beyond her child being abused. So the question is what will you tolerate? Are you on this grid at all? If you find yourself willing to tolerate anything on this grid, you are not ready for a relationship. You have to think of yourself in more of a respectable way beyond being abused. No one deserves to be abused and if the value that you have for yourself is not greater than this grid, it is best that you stay single.

      If you do not want to be another victim, you must accept that all of these categories represent abuse. The tolerance grid is just a small area of boundaries in regards to abuse, yet there are several other boundaries that do not necessarily revolve around abuse.

      Every healthy relationship has boundaries and in order to maintain a healthy relationship the both of you must communicate your likes and dislikes. Take the time to write down your dislikes. Be honest with yourself while writing. How do you want to be treated? By communicating what you like and dislike, a firm foundation of respect towards one another will be established. You cannot be disrespected by a loved one unless they blatantly disregard your boundaries and the only way they will know what your boundaries are is if you communicate what they are.

Now do not get me wrong. I am not encouraging you to become obsessive with this and detail every single dislike you have; some things are just common sense. For example, no one likes being lied to. If this is a deal breaker for you then definitely say so, but in all actuality lying is not welcome in a healthy relationship. Do not worry about what your partner will think about what you have written. And definitely do not sugarcoat your personal opinion. In all things be true. True to yourself and true to him. Now you do not necessarily have to show him the list of your boundaries, but it is essential for you to discuss them with him. He will never know what you like or dislike if you never say it to him. Setting boundaries can be for any relationship but it is primarily for relationships that have a future.

Setting boundaries is especially important when children are involved. Although this is your relationship, once you introduce a significant other to your children he becomes apart of their life too. You first have to decide whether or not you even want him to meet your children. Your children should not meet every man that you are dating. Why? Because children have a tendency of getting attached to people, especially young children. Right when they start to like Bob the two of you have broken up. This is not fair to your children and it sends them through another level of disappoint and abandonment. My recommendation is to not introduce him to them unless you are sure that this relationship will go further than just dating. This method will reduce the opportunities for disappointment.

One of the hardest things to do when you are in a new relationship after an abusive one is to reconnect with yourself. After being abused and mistreated for so long, we forget what our desires are and how we want to be treated. With that in mind it is always good to wait awhile before you start dating again and heal from the abuse that you have endured. Do not be so quick to fill that empty spot of loneliness. It is alright to be alone for awhile. If not to simply clear your mind of everything that has taken place. If you are filled with all the emotional baggage of past relationships, it will be difficult for you to set clear boundaries.

If you have a problem detailing your likes and dislikes, think of your daughter, sister or mother, how would you want them to be treated? More than likely, you would want them to be treated with the utmost respect and that is how you should be treated as well. Do not live in condemnation believing that you deserve what you can get...this is not true. The word condemnation means that you think of yourself as being unusable, worthless, undeserving. No matter what you have done in your past you have the absolute right to be respected and honored. Do not downplay your list of boundaries due to your idea of what you deserve in a relationship. You deserve the best! Not a bunch of drama and garbage. You have boundaries and you have the right to have those boundaries respected. And if he does not honor your boundaries then let him go.

WORDS
OF
FAITH

"Today, I am setting boundaries, not walls, in my relationships. I believe that God has created me to be respected and not disrespected. I will not ignore my boundaries in order to please other people. I will effectively communicate my likes and dislikes in order that my significant other will be aware of them. My boundaries are designed to empower me to be the woman God has called me to be and not a doormat. I will not waiver, ignore, or abandon the boundaries that are important to me and I expect other people to do the same."

Psalm 138:3 (NIV)

When I called, you answered me; you made me bold and stouthearted.

1 Corinthians 15:33 (NIV)

Do not be misled: "Bad company corrupts good character."

Psalm 118:6 (NIV)

The LORD is with me; I will not be afraid. What can man do to me?

Katha D. Blackwell

Not Another Victim

CHAPTER FAITH ELEVEN

One thing for sure that you must do regardless as to what relationship you are in is keep God first. As women we have a tendency of giving so much of ourselves to a man that we forget that we should truly give our all to God. It is easy to get off track when you are in love that is why I am encouraging you to not forget about God. Every relationship will come to an end at some time or another, yet the only relationship that will remain forever is your relationship with God. What is faith exactly? Faith is the substance of things hoped for and the evidence of things not seen (Hebrews 11:1).

Sometimes we can love people so much and

so hard that we abandon the One that loved us first. We put someone else in the place of Jesus when in actuality we should have kept Him first. This is a common theme that I have seen from women who are victims of abuse. Immediately when they get out of an abusive relationship they say, "I need to go back to church." Abusive relationships can lead you astray if you let them. On the other shoe there are women who constantly keep the faith in the midst of the abuse. I am talking to the women who have strayed away and have not kept the faith.

An abusive relationship has the tendency of beating the praise out of you to the point that you live in ultimate silence. This relationship is only there to steal and destroy what God has built on the inside of you...a lifestyle of worship. Everyone on this planet has a purpose and an abusive relationship is only there to distract you from where you should be and kill the very power God placed in you. I do not believe God ever intended for women to be abused. In Malachi chapter 2 verse 14, it is stated how the Lord does not hear the prayers of an abusive man and how he is disgusted with a man that is treacherous, meaning violent or hostile, towards his wife. Several married victims have told me they were trying to be a submissive wife according to the word of God. Take time to read Ephesians 5:21-33. A submissive wife is not supposed to be disrespected or intimidated. Submission is willingly allowing the husband to lead and direct the household while the wife puts his directions and requests first. In my opinion, women are fully equipped to have babies, run a household and run a business without the direction of a husband and I believe God knows that too and that is why we are called to submit to our husbands.

Recognizing how great and independent we are can lead our households into a world of chaos because there can only be one leader in the home. Women are absolutely capable of running their own home, for example God did not assign women a help meet. Eve did not need help, Adam needed help that's why God made Eve. I am not saying this to be haughty; this is to show you how God encourages wives, according to His word, in all our great abilities and talents to submit to our husbands. In other words, God is requesting wives to voluntarily humble themselves and serve someone that needs our help. The wife in no way, shape or fashion should be verbally or physically abused to submit. If the abuse is causing the wife to submit due to fear then she is really not submitting at all.

Submission is not produced out of fear...it is produced out of love. When a husband is truly good to his wife, she can easily submit to him out of love. If you were submissive because you were scared or believed he would do something then that is an indication that your submission was not true submission, rather it was intimidation.

Additionally, submission applies to wives... not girlfriends. If you are not married you have absolute free reign to run the show. This is where several women misinterpret the submissive scripture to be some universal relationship scripture. If you are not married, this scripture does not apply to your relationship. I do not care how long you have been dating or if he is the father of your children or even if you are engaged! If you are not married this scripture does not apply to you. Several victims have told me that they were trying to be submissive because the abuser would always quote this scripture, "Wives, submit to your husbands."Come to find out they were never married in the first place. If you are not married, you are not a wife and he is not a husband. You do not have to be submissive to your boyfriend. There is no scripture addressing boyfriends and girlfriends, so please stop listening to marriage scriptures that do not apply to you.

If your faith in God is an important factor in your life by all means follow the word regarding your actions and your relationships. Every relationship you have, whether it is intimate or blood-related, is either empowering you or discouraging you. Although you have been abused this is not what God had intended for your. Even if the abuser is a boyfriend, family member, etc. This is not how you should be treated. Usually in an abusive relationship the abuser will use the word of God to control and intimidate the victim. He misquotes the word and turns it into something it was never intended to be. The word of God describes our God-given rights as women and if we are not well informed of those rights we can easily be mislead by an abuser that claims to be a Christian. This faith section is intended to help you understand that you should never forget God loves you and that abuse is not Godly. Although you may have messed up, remember that God never intended for you to go through all the pain and abuse you have endured. The word of God says, "The thief cometh not, but to steal, and to kill, and to destroy: I am come that they might have life, and that they might have it more abundantly." John 10:10.

In order to not be another victim there are several factors that need to be considered when you are thinking about starting a new relationship:

#1: Should you be dating right now?

I am aware that you are an adult and have every right to date who you want whenever you want, but are you in a season to be dating? There

is nothing wrong with being single for awhile...
matter-of-fact when was the last time you spent
some considerable time being single? Do you need
to be in a relationship right now? Ask yourself that
question. If your answer is yes ask yourself why.
What causes you to think that you need to be in a
relationship at all? Possible answers..."Not getting
any younger", "My children need a father" or "I'm
just plain lonely". It is good to be honest with
yourself before getting into a relationship. When I
asked are you in a season to be dating, what I am
saying is that there is a season for everything. Just
like the weather changes and there is a time to
plant seeds in the ground there is another season
to harvest the plants that have grown. The same
thing goes for your life. There is a time and season
for everything under the sun. (Eccl. 3:1) So it is
good to know whether or not you should be
engaging in a relationship right now. Maybe you
should wait for awhile, yet if you decide to go
ahead and get into a relationship at this time
please continue to read the remaining factors.

#2: Salvation

If he is not saved, leave this man alone until
he gets saved. The Word of God tells us to not be
unequally yoked with unbelievers (2 Corinthians
6:14). What does this mean? For example, take two
horses drawing a carriage together. When horses

Katha D. Blackwell

are drawing a carriage together they are yoked up in other words bound together in order for the carriage to ride smoothly. If one of the horses is sluggish, too old, too fat, wild or unruly, then the carriage will not ride smoothly and the other horse will be doing most of the work...why? Because they are unequally yoked the two horses are not compatible with each other and it does not work.

An unsaved man has no business being with a saved woman. You love God and he does not. You confess and believe that Jesus is Lord and he does not. What can the two of you have in common if your love for God is not compatible? Although you may have his best interest in mind towards getting him saved what will be compromised along the way. If you meet a man that is absolutely the finest thing you have ever seen and he is not saved the best thing you can do for him is pray for him and then introduce him to some men of God at your church. Do not hook up with this man, do not date this man, and surely do not have sex with this man. Salvation should be the number one factor on your priority list.

For four years, I was over the Women's Ministry at a church in Illinois and one of the main questions I would ask the single women who started dating is the question of salvation... Is the man that you are dating saved? Do not settle for a man that is not saved all because you are not a perfect Christian. I have met a lot of Christian women who believe that since they do not live a life of holiness then they have no right to judge another person. I am not telling you to judge this man; I am encouraging you to use wisdom. Stop condemning yourself and settling for a man that does not know the one and only person that loves you more than anyone else...Jesus Christ. I'm done preaching...Let's move on to the next factor.

#3 Does He Practice What He Preaches?

If your man tells you that he is a man of God, then his lifestyle should reflect that. I am not saying that he has to be perfect, but what I am saying is that his actions should match up with his words. The Word of God tells us to not only be hearers of the word but to be doers of the word also (James 1:22). A man that follows the good words that come out of his mouth is the kind of man deserving of your time. He needs to be a man of his word. Many women get involved with a man all because he can quote the bible. Quoting the bible is what many people do, including the devil. Do not be impressed by a man that can quote the bible, especially if you are not studying the word of God for yourself. If you are not studying the word of God for yourself, you are truly setting yourself up for a wolf in sheep's clothing. It does not matter what his professional or social status is. He could be a pastor, minister, teacher, preacher and could end up an abuser. So please know the word for yourself and watch to see if this man practices what he preaches.

#4 **Build You Up or Tear You Down.**

Does interacting with him cause you to fall into sin? Is he encouraging you to do something that you know is wrong? If you answered yes to any of these questions, then this relationship is tearing you down. The men in our life should be building us up, not tearing us down. You can do bad all by yourself. A relationship that is building you up is one that encourages you to pray, to show honor to God through your relationship, that respects your set boundaries. A healthy relationship will not conflict with your relationship with God. Although you may be madly in love with this person are you willing to compromise your morals and values for him? These are the kind of questions you should ask yourself when it comes to your relationship with this man. As I stated at the beginning of this chapter, the only relationship that you have that will last forever is your relationship with God. All relationships will pass away, but the one that is most important is the one you have with God while you are still on this earth. You have to maintain your relationship with God before you get to heaven. Why would you move in with someone you know nothing about? On a better note, why would anyone move you into their home when they do not know you? That is how we have to think about how important it is to maintain our relationship with God and not get off track with the temporary love here on earth.

WORDS
OF
FAITH

"No man or relationship comes before my relationship with God. God is my everything, my friend, my all and all, so pleasing Him is my priority. I am no longer consumed with the idea of marriage. I trust that the man for me will find me at the appointed time. I will not get into a relationship with any man that does not love God, is not saved or does not strive to live a sin free life. From this day forth, I will listen to Godly wisdom from my family, friends and my children. Today, I ignore every emotion of loneliness, insecurity, untrustworthiness, fear and I rest in the peace of God, the joy of God, the love of God and I believe that everything will work out for my good."

Deuteronomy 6:5 (NIV)
Love the LORD your God with all your heart and with all your soul and with all your strength

Psalm 97:10 (NIV)
Let those who love the LORD hate evil, for he guards the lives of his faithful ones and delivers them from the hand of the wicked.

Mark 11:22-23 (NIV)
"Have faith in God," Jesus answered."Truly I tell you, if anyone says to this mountain, 'Go, throw yourself into the sea,' and does not doubt in their heart but believes that what they say will happen, it will be done for them.

Katha D. Blackwell

Not Another Victim

THE CHILDREN

The easiest way to know whether or not the person you are dating is the person to be with is to introduce him to your children after you have decided to get serious with him. Serious in the sense of marriage, not sex or moving in with each other. If you do not want to get serious with this man, by all means do not introduce him to your family. Children at times can easily get attached to a man that is not their father, especially if their father is not actively in the picture. At the same time, depending on their age, children can discern the wrong man a mile away. I believe children are born with a natural discernment unless it has been stripped from them. Most children are not trying to be mean when they show their discomfort when approached for a hug or a kiss. Allow your child to show affection to whomever they feel comfortable showing affection to. This will strengthen their trust in their gut feeling and will help them as adults to discern. Forcing them to like someone or hug someone is not the way for them to learn discernment.

In the event that your child is uncomfortable with this person, regardless as to who it is, do not ignore your child's reaction. Do not get me wrong I am not telling you to allow your children to choose your man, but at least allow them to give you honest feedback regarding this man. If he turns out to be the wrong man, you are not the only person that is going to have to put up with his abuse, your children will also. Do you honestly think your children want to see you hurt? Of course not, they want to see you happy. So before you decide to engage your children into a long relationship allow them to participate in your decision to be with this man.

Before you start dating, find out how your children feel about you dating. Your child may have some anxiety about you dating and the only way you would know that is by setting up an opportunity for them to honestly tell you how they feel. Let me just stop and say that if your relationship with your child is not strong and healthy, then you should not even think about getting into a relationship. Your relationship with your child needs to heal before you start fresh with someone else, especially if you have young children under 12. The level of trauma your child has experienced is far more important than fulfilling your needs.

Another reason to check with your children before starting to date is for their own safety. I have heard many stories about how the "new" boyfriend was molesting the children. Once you start allowing someone into your home you are giving this person free reign into the lives of your children. This is not meant to scare you; rather I am trying to get you to come to a full understanding of how careful you should be when dating.

Another important factor to remember is to never introduce your date to your family during the honeymoon stage of the relationship. Every relationship, whether it is intimate or not, goes through a honeymoon stage. The honeymoon stage is when everyone is nice, well-mannered, on time, well-groomed and agrees with everything. After that comes the real you and the real him, during which the two of you should have at least one real disagreement. Once you have had your first real argument then you will have a clear view of the kind of person you are dealing with. There is no point in introducing your family and your children to someone who will be around for a few days, weeks, or months. Everyone does not deserve the privilege to meet your children...no matter how cute or how bad your children are. Listed below are a couple questions you should ask yourself before bringing him home to meet your children and family:

#1: Do you know this man?

This is a real question you should ask yourself. Do you KNOW him? Where is he from? Does he have children? Has he been to jail? Has/does he do drugs? Is he married? Has he ever been married? Does he work? Where does he live? Where are his parents? Where are his siblings? Take an hour or so and look him up on the internet. There are several things you can find out about a person on the internet. If he has ever been convicted you can find this out within your state. A lot of information is available to the public. Even if you have a not so squeaky clean background, still take the initiative to find information about this man. Regardless as to how much mess you have been in the goal is to move forward and not backward with your life and make sure that this man is safe to be around your family.

#2: Is the relationship serious?

There is absolutely no point in introducing him to your family if he is not sure about the relationship. Has he told you where he wants this relationship to go? If so, how serious is he about this relationship? Possibly marriage? Or what? If he merely wants to hang-out for awhile, then hang-out for awhile. There is no point in pushing the relationship in a direction that he is not ready for.

Once you have decided to introduce him to your family, consider the following in order to make the best of the first visit:

#1: Set a time for the children to meet him

You should never just bring this man over to meet your children. This is a no-no. Their first initial meeting should be something that is planned with both, the children and him, being informed. The first impression is the last, so it is important to make the first encounter meaningful. Make it special. Set it up so that both parties can enjoy the time spent. For example, maybe you could have a movie night at your house and invite him over. Or maybe go out to eat together allowing the children to ask him questions and allow him to interact with them. Never leave your children alone with this man. Not because he could be unsafe, but because he is new to the family and although you know him, your children do not. He is still considered a stranger so please keep that in mind. The time they spend together, with you present, will give you a better view of how all this can work out.

Number 2: Let your children be themselves

This is not an opportunity to sell your children to him like some cheap car salesman saying,"See they're not so bad". Children are not a burden, so do not start to think about how no one wants a woman with children. Truth be told it is a major step to take, but being in the life of a child is a blessing, not a curse. So do not make them act in a way that is not the way they normally act. In other words, don't try to impress him. Even though you want him to like them, just let everything flow naturally. If he doesn't like your children for who they are is he really a keeper? Resist the urge to force your children to like him or be liked by him. Your children are the prize not him and by now he should know that if he wants you he has to accept all of you, which includes your children. Do not give in to the feeling of desperation because you have children. There are plenty of men out there who love children and the right man for you will love them.

Your family is an essential part of your life and I encourage you to include them in your selection of the next man you date. They do not need to make the decision for you, yet it is important that someone who loves and cares about you gives you good feedback about this man. This may be hard for women who do not have positive, caring family members. If this is the case for you, go to your pastor or a dear friend and ask for advice. Someone that loves you can give you the feedback you need so seek out that feedback.

WORDS
OF
FAITH

I will seek wisdom, direction and advice from caring family and friends. I will not allow my desires to disregard my children's emotions or concerns. I will not get involved with a man who does not respect me or my children. I will not be desperate for a man in my life, I will not be desperate to get married, I will not make my children try to impress him. I will wait and trust that the Lord knows what's best for me and as I follow his plan for my life, the right man will find me.

Psalm 56:11 (NIV)

In God I trust and am not afraid. What can man do to me?

Exodus 20:12 (NIV)

Honor your father and your mother, so that you may live long in the land the LORD your God is giving you

Katha D. Blackwell

DISAGREEMENTS

Everyone in this world has had or will have a disagreement with another person at some point in their life. I define a disagreement as a discussion with differing points of view. You probably have had a few disagreements throughout your life and will have more. Every healthy relationship has a disagreement, yet it is the attitude behind the disagreement that makes the disagreement either healthy or abusive. Please note that a disagreement is not the same as a fight, although it can turn into one, a disagreement is not necessarily a fight. Once you decide to begin another relationship, do not be afraid to have a

155

disagreement with him. Disagreements are a natural part of life and should be welcomed into a healthy relationship. What kind of relationship would you have if you never disagreed about anything? That would be a fake relationship...all smiles no frowns. A truly healthy relationship consists of real people, real emotions and real words. If you have any hope of keeping this relationship going strong, both of you must be honest and real with each other. Take off the masks that come in a new relationship and be real with each other.

There is a season in every new relationship that consists of a lot of fluff. When I say fluff I mean a lot of lovey-dovey, hugs and kisses, "I love you so much", "your perfect", "we're perfect", "you can do no wrong", etc. And then reality sets in and all the things you thought you were fades away. New relationships are like new jobs. At the beginning you arrive on time, are never late, finish all assignments, are respectable to co-workers and customers and then after a few months you get comfortable and start showing your true colors. This is the same thing that takes place in a relationship. It is not that people are deliberately trying to be fake, it is just everyone's goal is to make a good impression. Once we get comfortable our real flaws come out. Everybody does this. You may start your relationship by wearing perfume

and your hair is always done, but as soon as you get comfortable you start slacking in these areas. A lot men do the same thing. They start out clean cut, shaved, shoes polished and cologne, next thing you know they never get their hair cut and they wear the same old outfit every week.
Although this level of realness may leave a bitter taste in your mouth, all relationships go through this transition. The transition of real emotions, real responses and instead of sugar coating, words come straight out. With this transition of actions, a disagreement will eventually arise.
The one thing to keep in mind is that everyone argues at some point.

Do not assume that he is abusive all because you have a disagreement with him. It is expected that you may jump to the conclusion that he is an abuser, but before you do please recognize the signs. If you find yourself feeling intimidated or feel uncomfortable during the disagreement, express your feelings towards him. In other words...communicate your emotions. This man is not psychic and may not know the history of your relationships, so do not assume he should know how to approach you during a disagreement. Additionally, everyone has been raised differently so what was appropriate in your family may not be the same in his family. All new relationships go through a stage of getting to know each other. This is a healthy stage as long as both of you are honest and open.

In the event that he says or does something that you do not like, you should tell him. Once you have expressed your feelings towards his approach (*if he is worth keeping*) he will apologize and adjust his actions. If he brushes you off and starts to act like you provoked him to act that way *then* you can start to think that this man may not be the one for you. An argument becomes abusive once physical abuse or verbal abuse begins. Now please note that the goal of arguing is not to see if he is abusive, rather it is an opportunity to see how the both of you act when a disagreement arrives. Will you be true or will you sugarcoat your words? Are you loud or are you quiet? Are you able to receive criticism without taking it personal? This section is not encouraging you to start disagreements with him. That would not be wise. The point I am making is for you to not jump to the conclusion that a disagreement means abuse. It does not.

A disagreement turns abusive once name-calling, intimidation, threatening and disrespect enter into the room. For example, if you are called stupid, ignorant, fat, slow, ugly, etc., then you are being verbally abused. This is not good and should not be tolerated. Even if it gets to the point where you both are calling each other names it is still unacceptable. Even if this is the first disagreement, you have the choice to either address his behavior and let him know that his behavior will not be tolerated or you can just extinguish the relationship completely.

There are men out there that will change their actions to your liking once they are aware of your dislikes. If he really wants to remain in the relationship, he should immediately change his behavior or at least try to change. There are no excuses once he has been informed of your dislikes. If he begins to make excuses for why he keeps doing what you dislike then it is clear to say that you do not have a man on your hands...he is a boy. Real men will not constantly make excuses for their actions. Real men own up to their actions and change. There is no need to stay in a relationship with a man that never accepts responsibility for his actions.

This kind of relationship can become draining and tiresome. You will constantly be pointing out his faults and he will never accept his faults. I encourage you to not settle for a man that disregards your feelings. He needs to be 10 times better than previous boyfriends not just a little better. As I stated in previous chapters, set up new boundaries that reflect a healthy relationship. Do not allow the thought of loneliness or fear lead you into staying with a man that does not honor your boundaries.

During various group counseling sessions, I asked the question does loneliness outweigh being abused? Some women said that they rather be abused than be lonely. If you find yourself agreeing with this, just remember that being with an abusive man really is being alone. It is better to be alone and happy than unhappy with a house full of people. But if this is a major concern of yours then it is important that you engage yourself in healthy activities at church or within your community to fill the feeling of loneliness.

No one wants an unhealthy relationship and allowing actions like these to linger in your relationship will surely tear it apart. Either you will gradually be hurt or he will gradually be hurt, either way the atmosphere of your relationship is slowly but surely turning in the wrong direction.

When my husband and I began to tell our parents about our relationship, his mother asked a very important question. She asked if we had ever argued with each other? Our response was "No, of course not." She then told us to check how strong our love was after an argument, because a disagreement will test how much you really love someone. O, boy was she right! Once we had our first argument we were able to clearly see whether or not we wanted to stay together. And it was good for my husband to know that when I argue I get loud. And it was good for me to know that when he argues he does not like to be interrupted, something I do often. Disagreeing made us more aware of each other.

Every relationship usually starts in the Honeymoon phase where everything is wonderful and no one can do any wrong. This phase is not a true representation of a healthy relationship. It is more like a puppy love phase and both parties are perfect, when in fact neither party is perfect at all. This is where the perfect masks are taken off and for a brief moment you get to see the true person behind all that love and perfection. The key thing is that both people are mature enough to acknowledge when they are wrong and brave enough to admit it. The question is will you express your difference of opinion? Due to past relationships, some women will try very hard to avoid a disagreement because of fear. Fear that he will leave. Fear that you will find yourself back in another bad relationship. Now is not the time to operate in fear, now is the time to walk by faith in every situation and step out. You have nothing to lose but time, so let's make the best of today and be real and honest.

WORDS
OF
FAITH

"I recognize that although everyone is different, the Holy Spirit does not change and neither does God. As differences of opinion arise in my relationship, I declare that a greater level of communication and understanding will come to both of us. I confess that I will not get into my flesh when I feel disrespected rather I will operate in the gifts of the spirit which represents order and peace. I will use discernment to determine whether or not the discussion is getting out of hand. I will communicate effectively when I feel disrespected and with all boldness I will speak my mind in a kind and confident manner."

Galatians 5:22-23 (NIV)

But the fruit of the Spirit is love, joy, peace,
patience, kindness, goodness, faithfulness,
gentleness and self-control. Against such things
there is no law.

Jeremiah 17:7 (NIV)

But blessed is the man who trusts in the LORD,
whose confidence is in him.

Not Another Victim

Katha D. Blackwell

CHAPTER

SEX

FOURTEEN

Although sexual intercourse may be important in your relationship it is important to know that sex does not have to be apart of your premarital relationship. Sex was specifically made for marriage, not for unmarried people. I am aware that not everyone believes that, but before we go any further let me make it clear that premarital sex is sin. If you are expecting intimacy in your relationship, please know that sex is not the definition of intimacy and affection. Sex is not something that is just thrown around to any willing vessel that wants a piece of your good loving. Sex is something to be given willingly and with love and not a means to save a relationship or to be used out of force. In order to protect yourself, develop boundaries regarding your sexual willingness. If you are celibate or waiting until you get married or are just not interested in having sex, tell the person you are dating. Whichever way you decide to go, sex or not, is totally up to you. I'm not trying to preach, just stick to whatever your decision is and let him know early on in the relationship.

If it appears that your new partner has a problem respecting your views then it is important that you all discuss your feelings even more. If he does not comprehend your beliefs and tries to persuade you that making love is a way to show your love, there is a good chance that he will not be able to hold out until you are good and ready and if that is the case let him go. The last thing you want to do is try to keep a man by doing something you are not comfortable with or have made yourself comfortable with. This is not healthy. We show people that we love them everyday and it does not involve having sex. Abusers use tactics to make the victim feel as though her decision is the wrong decision. This action leads many women to believe there view is wrong and causes them to waiver from their original stance.

If you are married and have been a victim of abuse in the past, again communicating your sexual desires or dislikes is important. In all marriages you should be able to openly and honestly tell your spouse when you feel uncomfortable with certain sexual acts or positions. Now do not get me wrong all married couples should have sex. And if you are not having sex with your spouse you both need to find out why. My point here is to inform you that any and all sexual acts should be done willingly and lovingly. If you do not like oral or anal sex then you should say so. If you do not like role playing then you should say so, etc. etc. Whatever you are uncomfortable doing you should discuss this with your spouse and they should honor your feelings until your feelings change.

Being married and sexual abuse has always been a tricky area. Some women may have a problem identifying whether or not the physical pressure their husband put on them to have sex was acceptable. There may be some women who were raped by their husbands yet did not see it as rape. Rape is rape. Whether you are married or not. Any form of physical pressure or force on you to have sex is unacceptable. If you want to be submissive to your spouse understand that submission is one thing and rape is another. Please do not put rape and submission in the same category this is again is unacceptable. If your husband has physically forced himself on you, then you are in an abusive relationship and it is best to acknowledge that fact now and deal with it now. In the back of this book are several resources and free hotline numbers that you can call for help. The best thing you can do to get out of the situation you are in is to reach out and talk to someone who can help you.

Your feelings towards sex are important in your relationship. Whether you agree or not with everything I have mentioned in this chapter, my point is that you must communicate your feelings about sex and not waiver regardless as to how cute or sexy your man is.

WORDS
OF
FAITH

"*My body is a temple of God. I will not allow my body to be the pleasure playground for anyone unless it is for my husband. I believe that God ordained sex for marriage and with that belief I have the strength to abstain from pre-marital sex. My body is to be respected therefore no one has the right to do anything to it that I object to. Today, I rededicate my body to the Lord and resist every ounce of lust, fornication and sin that tries to tempt me. Today, I present my body a living sacrifice before God and my desire is to be holy and acceptable before Him.*"

1 Corinthians 6:18 (NIV)

Flee from sexual immorality. All other sins a man commits are outside his body, but he who sins sexually sins against his own body.

Romans 12:1 (NIV)

Therefore, I urge you, brothers, in view of God's mercy, to offer your bodies as living sacrifices, holy and pleasing to God—this is your spiritual act of worship.

1 Corinthians 7:4 (KJV)

The wife hath not power of her own body, but the husband: and likewise also the husband hath not power of his own body, but the wife.

Katha D. Blackwell

Not Another Victim

LOVE

For some of you a new relationship will easily come into place. For example, let's say you met the right man and so far things have been going well. But before things go any further let us talk about what your relationship will consist of and whether or not this new man fulfills the requirements of the man you deserve.

It is easy to say, "I Love You", but what do you actually mean when you say that? Love is more than just lip service; it is followed by an action. How do you love yourself? Do you speak positive things about yourself? You should always speak good things to someone you love and if you love yourself you should speak positive things to yourself. As you build your relationship with God you will learn more and more of how you should be loved by someone. The only way I can explain to you how you should be loved is by expressing the love God has for you.

For starters let's figure out what love is? In order to be in love with someone, you must first know what love is. The word of the Lord says that God is love(1 John 4:8). Now if you do not know God or do not have a relationship with Him then it will be difficult for you to know how to love or how to be loved. How amazing it is to love someone that you have never seen with your natural eye, yet still love Him out of faith. The most important relationship for you to have is a relationship with the Lord. Before you even start dating you should first renew your relationship with Him. One thing that I have seen several women do wrong is get into a relationship with another man without first improving their relationship with the Lord. A relationship with the Lord is the most perfect relationship you will ever have. Not only will you learn about what a healthy relationship looks like, but you will also improve your discernment regarding which man is right and which one is wrong. Your relationship with God will guide you into the right direction regarding the right man for you.

God wants you to be in a healthy relationship that represents His holy covenant with you. A relationship filled with holy, unconditional love that will last a lifetime. Not some cheap, one-night stand love that wastes your time and emotions. After several miserable relationships isn't it time to finally have a good man that is the real deal 100% and not just 50%. You want a man that will love you the way the Lord does. You deserve a good man. You have been through enough drama, now is the time to have a relationship that is filled with patience, peace and most of all the love of God. Your feelings of loneliness will slowly be minimized as you strengthen your relationship with the Lord.

It is not your job to look for your next husband, it is his job to find you(Prov. 18:22). Additionally, throughout the word of God, real women did not look for a man. They were merely being obedient to their parents and to God when their husband found them. The only women who were looking for men were harlots and prostitutes. Real women did not go out looking for a man. When you are loving on God and improving your relationship with Him, you are destined for greatness not only with a new relationship, but with your career, future, and family. There are several benefits to strengthening your relationship with God. Now is the time to move forward with your life forgetting about your past experiences and finally experience real love.

One of the many things women struggle with is the desire to be loved by somebody. Regardless as to whether that somebody is a relative or a friend we all want to be loved, adored and admired. God shows us unconditional love everyday. He loves us when we make mistakes. He loves us even when we don't talk to Him for weeks. He has that pure unconditional love that we seek from people. Throughout the new testament of the bible there are several examples showing how Jesus Christ came to heal people who were broken-hearted, living in sin, in bondage, etc. (Luke 4:18). Christ came for people who were imperfect not for people who had it all together. If you have a sex problem, He came for you. If you have a drug problem, He came for you. If you have a money problem, He came for you. If you have a sin problem of any kind, He came for you and He loves you. All you have to do is come to Him, just the way you are. Do not try to get perfect first because you will never perfect yourself without God in your life. As you improve your relationship with Love, aka God, you will gradually change. The word of God tells us to be transformed by the renewing of our mind (Romans 12:2). The word transformed means to be changed. If you want change in your life, then you must change the way you think about your life. Taking a new look at every situation, trial, test or situation that comes your way will help you have a better outcome in your life. And the more time you spend with God praying and talking to Him the better off you will be.

In all our relationships it is important that we know who love is. If the man you are dating does not know God for himself then how does he know how to love you. He does not. And although he may be the best man you have ever met that means nothing if he does not know and have a relationship with God. This is one of the main things that you should be focused on when engaging in a relationship with a new man.

Once you make the decision to date again, there is one thing that must be certain of this new man...he must be saved. He must confess and believe that Jesus Christ died on the cross and rose to life again. What is the point of getting involved with a man that is not a man of faith? He will not understand the love you have for God and may question why you go to church, pray, etc. And is this really the kind of man you want to be involved with? Hopefully not.

The word of God tells us to not be unequally yoked with unbelievers(2 Corinthians 6:14). In other words, do not be in a commitment with someone that does not believe in God. If your faith means anything to you, you will avoid getting into a relationship with a man that is not saved. The reasons are endless even if he has all the right qualities, this is not the man for you until he gets saved. And even then when he gets saved, going to church every Sunday is not enough. He needs to have a solid relationship with God.

Many women have asked me how can you tell if he is the real deal? Here are the things you should do and look for to confirm that this man is the real deal:

Number 1: Know the word for yourself

One of the many problems that arise when a woman is dating the wrong man is that he manipulates the word of God to get what he wants. For example, some men will use the scripture, "Wives submit to your husbands.."(Ephesians 5:22) in order to get his wife to do what he says. If you have not read this entire chapter in Ephesians you will not know that there is more to this scripture than what is being presented.

Once you read this chapter you will know that submitting is not something done by force. It is a willingness on the wife's end to support and follow through with the desires of her husband. The key word is willingness in other words you are willing to submit and want to submit. I could give several more examples, yet the point I am making is for you to know the word of God for yourself to decrease the opportunity for manipulation.

If you are not studying the word for yourself there are several ways anyone can manipulate the word in order to control and intimidate you. If you ever find your man misquoting the word to get his way, check him and his words and inform him of the truth. Let him know that you are not ignorant to the word of God nor are you a fool.

Number 2: Practice what he preaches

I cannot stress this enough...If he is always quoting scripture then he needs to practice what he is preaching. He cannot live one way with you and another way with people at church, work or with family. He should be consistent and believe in what he is preaching. If he is leading you to sin, then there is a good chance that he is not the man for you. Bottom-line he needs to be a man of his word.

Number 3: He should show love

He cannot be a real deal 100% man of God unless he shows love. Love beyond the bedroom. I'm talking about that Christ kind of love. If he constantly is quoting scripture, but not showing any compassion or love towards people then he is just a bunch of talk. The word of God tells us that if we do not have love our actions are nothing (1 Corinthians 13). A woman that visited my church told the story of how she knew her husband was the one. She placed his name in the scripture in place of the word love. Bobby is patient, Bobby is kind, Bobby does not boast, etc. This is the same thing you should do with any prospective man you are dating. Is he patient? Is he kind? Does he boast? These are the kind of questions you should ask yourself in regards to the character of this man.

Lastly, remember this point. If no one ever tells you that you are special, God says you are special. If no one ever says I love you, God says, "I love you". God's love for you, no matter who you are, is the kind of love we all want. And if you are the kind of person who wants God's love, then expect for this new man in your life to show that kind of love to you. There is no reason to settle for a man that will not give you the love you deserve. I am in no way trying to sound snooty, but isn't it time for you to experience true love? The answer is yes. You deserve it no matter what you have done or what you will do tomorrow, you deserve to be loved.

WORDS
OF
FAITH

"*Today, I acknowledge that I deserve to be loved. The Lord loves me more than anyone on this earth. The Lord loves me. The Lord loves me. And I love Him. I declare that my heart is filled with love and not hate. I declare that anyone who loves me must love me the way Christ loves the church. I will not settle for a temporary love rather I welcome Godly love.*"

1 John 4:8 (NIV)

Whoever does not love does not know God,
because God is love.

1 Corinthians 13:4-7 (NIV)

Love is patient, love is kind. It does not envy, it
does not boast, it is not proud. It is not rude, it is
not self-seeking, it is not easily angered, it keeps
no record of wrongs. Love does not delight in evil
but rejoices with the truth. It always protects,
always trusts, always hopes, always perseveres.

Katha D. Blackwell

Not Another Victim

STEP 4
Recognize Red Flags

Not Another Victim

VERBAL ABUSE

This section is designed to help you identify various kinds of abuse. First I will talk about verbal abuse. Verbal abuse can be defined as any form of vocalization used to intimidate, belittle or hurt another person.

One of the most abusive actions that are highly overlooked is verbal abuse. You know that old saying, "sticks and stones may break my bones but words will never hurt me", well that is a lie. Words do hurt and remain longer than physical abuse. Words are very powerful.

As the bible states in Proverbs 18:21, Life and Death are in the power of the tongue. Not in the power of the fist or the hand, but in the tongue. That little member of your mouth has great power because through your mouth comes your reality. The words that are spoken to you can turn into a reality for you. How many times were you called stupid, fat or even ugly? How often do you put yourself down in these areas? Maybe you make comments like…"I'm not smart enough" or "I'm no beauty queen". Who put those thoughts there? Better yet who let those thoughts in? The way you think about yourself becomes a reality. The bible says so a man thinketh so is he (Proverbs 23:7), in other words the way you think about yourself is what you become. If you constantly think that you won't make it by yourself…you won't.

Verbal abuse can play in your head over and over again whereas the physical wounds will heal. It is essential that you quickly check and acknowledge when someone is trying to put you down. Not necessarily in an attitude or disrespectful way, but do not entertain negativity. I am not going to go through every aspect of verbal abuse. What I will do is provide a short list describing various forms of verbal abuse and provide a description and an example. This is only to help you recognize and know what verbal abuse is.

Listed are a few forms of verbal abuse:

1. <u>Intimidation</u>: Abuser uses words or facial expressions to make the victim feel as though she will be harmed if she does not follow his orders. The facial expressions are similar to the expressions a parent would give a child.

Example: Bill gives Marie "the look" right after she smiles and speaks to a male co-worker.

2. <u>Name-Calling</u>: Abuser uses words to belittle the victim.

Example: Bill tells Marie she is stupid for not wearing a warmer coat.

3. <u>Withholding</u>: Abuser does not share information about himself or his feelings with the victim, yet expects the victim to withhold nothing from him.

Example: Although Bill has had a bad day at work, he will not tell Marie why he is so upset, instead he makes her feel as though she has done something wrong.

Now there are several ways in which verbal abuse can take place and all three of the areas listed touch base with all forms of verbal abuse. In order for you not to become a victim, you cannot remain with a verbally abusive man. These words will truly tear you apart if you remain. Even if it does not turn physically abusive, the tearing apart of your character and your spirit will be brutally hurt. If you are currently in an abusive relationship and are not sure as to whether or not your relationship is abusive, I encourage you to take the time and go to your local library and search for books with the topic of verbal abuse.

WORDS
OF
FAITH

"Today, I acknowledge that verbal abuse is wrong and not acceptable. Words have power therefore I will not accept negative words spoken to me nor will I speak negative words towards myself. I rebuke every negative word that has been spoken to me and I receive and believe that I am strong, beautiful, smart, mighty woman of God! I will not accept any man that is verbally abusive. I do not believe that God wants me to be abused in any way, therefore I will not tolerate being verbally abused."

Proverbs 18:21 (NIV)
The tongue has the power of life and death,
and those who love it will eat its fruit.

Philippians 4:13 (NIV)
I can do everything through him who gives me
strength.

Katha D. Blackwell

Not Another Victim

PHYSICAL ABUSE

Another area of abuse that, in my opinion, is most common is physical abuse. Physical Abuse is anything that is used to do harm to the physical well-being of another person. For example, if the abuser were to push you this would be considered physical abuse. Another example is if the abuser locked you outside of the house this too would be considered physical abuse. A common thing that I have seen among victims of abuse is the idea that certain forms of abuse are okay or are not really abusive. The truth of the matter is that anytime someone tries to physically harm you it should be considered physical abuse. As stated in the boundaries chapter, every woman has a level of tolerance that they have regarding physical abuse. The goal of this chapter is to keep you aware of what physical abuse looks like. This will help you in identifying an abusive action. Listed below are several different forms of physical abuse:

Sexual Abuse: The word "No" is still valid in every situation that comes, so in the event that a woman says "No" to any sexual act and the sexual act is forced this could be considered sexual abuse. The same thing goes for women who are not married. Regardless as to whether it is a husband, a boyfriend or fiancé, sexual abuse is never acceptable.

Punching: Regardless as to whether it was with an open fist or a closed fist punching is still considered abuse. The punch does not necessarily have to be in the face only. It can be on any part of the body.

Kicking: Whether or not the abuser has shoes on when he kicks you or no shoes at all. Kicking is still kicking.

Slapping: If the slap was a light tap or a full force backhand. This is still abuse. Do not worry as to whether or not the slap left a bruise. This is still abuse

Threatening to Kill: If he threatens to kill you this too can be considered physical abuse.

Or rather threatening to use physical abuse. **Hitting with a Weapon:** If he uses a belt or any other item to harm you with, then this too is physical abuse. There are several descriptions of physical abuse that I could list here, however I believe you understand the general examples.

Physical abuse in no way should be taken lightly. Regardless as to whether or not he apologizes the next day or hour, understand that if he is slapping you today, he may be punching you tomorrow and killing you the day after that.

Although there are several forms of abuse outside of verbal and physical, the most obvious forms are verbal and physical. Please keep in mind that any form of abuse is wrong no matter how frequent or infrequent. Without being physically abused there are various signs that are red flags in regards to a potentially abusive man. We will discuss red flags in the next chapter.

WORDS
OF
FAITH

"No form of physical abuse is acceptable, therefore I will not accept an abusive relationship. From this day forward I am no longer a victim, rather I am victorious because I have overcome every abuse that has been in my life and every pain that has brought me down. I will never be physically abused again. I will never be physically abused again. I will never be physically abused again. I declare that my children will not be in abusive relationships and that every relationship I connect with is filled with the peace and love of God."

Isaiah 54:17 (KJV)

No weapon that is formed against thee shall prosper; and every tongue that shall rise against thee in judgment thou shalt condemn. This is the heritage of the servants of the LORD, and their righteousness is of me, saith the LORD.

Not Another Victim

RED FLAGS

CHAPTER EIGHTEEN

If you really want to avoid being in a bad relationship, you must recognize red flags when they come. Red flags are actions or sayings he may say or do that give you a hint that this man may be an abuser. Red flags are not easily sighted unless you are looking. For example, if your boyfriend calls or texts you 20 times in one day just to check up on you would you consider that a red flag? As a teenager, I thought this was cute, but this is a red flag. Sure 20 times a day may sound like he really likes you, but what happens when he starts to call 30-40 times and although you have told him where you are and what you are doing this is not enough. This is a red flag. Here is a list of red flags that

should not go unnoticed:
- Calling or texting you constantly throughout the day while you are at work, school or at home
- Telling you what to wear and what not to wear
- Isolating you from your friends and family. He may say, " I want to spend more time with you."
- Making decisions on your behalf without consulting you

These are just a few examples of red flags. All red flags are connected to Power and Control. Abusers want to take away your power by controlling your actions and decisions.

No abuser is a particular race, color, height or weight. They do not carry around signs saying, "Hey, I'm an Abuser!" Some are rich and some are poor, but the only thing they have in common is that they all act alike. It's as if they had their own manual on how to be abusive. Listed below are a few traits that most abusers present:
- Controlling
- Insecure
- Bad communicator
- Double-personality (Lovable then A Nightmare)
- Lies
- Never accepts responsibility for his

own actions
- Shifts Blame
- Keeps secrets as if they are for your good
- Violent
- Aggressive or sometimes passive aggressive
- Sexist-Macho personality by demeaning women
- Has a way of making you think you are losing your mind
- Jealousy

These are just a few characteristics that most abusers show. But the one thing to keep in mind is that if you have a gut feeling that something is not right with this man, go with your gut. Regardless as to whether or not he fits into any of these characteristics. Also, keep in mind that abusers do not see themselves as abusers. So if you decide you want to ask him about any past abuse he may have done, please know that what is abusive to him may not be abusive to you.

Lastly, the best way to avoid an abuser is to use the gut feeling God gave you, this is known as discernment. If something tells you that something is not right with this man, follow that gut-feeling. Regardless as to how nice he is, follow your gut. It will save you from getting involved with this kind of man.

WORDS
OF
FAITH

"My discernment is sharp and with the Holy Spirit leading me, I can spot an abuser a mile away. I trust that the Lord will lead me to avoid abusive men. Today, I have a clear understanding of how I am supposed to be treated regardless as to what the world says. The next relationship I get into will be with a man who is in his right mind. I am not impressed with a jealous attitude. I will quickly recognize a red flag and not ignore it. My life is worth more than being with an abusive man and I will not settle for less."

<u>Proverbs 29:22 (NIV)</u>
An angry man stirs up dissension, and a hot-
tempered one commits many sins.

<u>Proverbs 22:24-26 (NIV)</u>
Do not make friends with a hot-tempered man, do
not associate with one easily angered, or you may
learn his ways and get yourself ensnared.

Not Another Victim

Katha D. Blackwell

Not Another Victim

STEP 5

Deciding to Leave

Not Another Victim

GETTING OUT

In the event that after reading this book you come to the conclusion that you are in a bad relationship, this last chapter is designed to help you get out of the situation safely when you are ready:

#1 Decide whether or not you are going to stay with him or leave him. This is the biggest and most dangerous decision you will make. This is not an easy decision to make although it should be. It is expected for you to have some doubts about leaving so do not think something is wrong with you. If you are still in love with him, which most women usually are, take some time to think about which part of him you are still in love with. The man that you are in love with may not exist anymore. It's okay to still be in love with this man, but that does not mean that you should stay with him at this time. If you are in danger, it is best for you to be in a safe place. Take some time to think about this and plan carefully.

#2 Talk to someone you can trust and inform them of the situation. Do not be surprised if this person does not fully understand what is going on. Family and friends usually go into rescue mode when they are aware they see you in danger. So if they give you an attitude or are upset with this whole situation, don't shut them out. It is natural for loved ones to feel this way. Just tell them what you plan to do.

#3 Contact the National Domestic Violence Hotline at **1-800-799-7233** and discuss your options

#4 Make copies of everything such as birth certificates, social security cards, car keys, house keys, IDs, etc.

#5 Contact your Pastor as long as he will be supportive. If your pastor is telling you to stay with an abusive husband, then it is clear that he does not understand the danger that you are in. This is of no fault of his own it's just there are numerous pastors who make light of domestic violence and are more focused on keeping the family together. Your safety comes first and once your spouse decides to put your safety last then it is time to go.

#6 Pack an extra bag of clothing and store it at a friend's house.

#7 Seek counseling for yourself. Most domestic violence counseling is free. You can call the hotline in #3 for counseling in your area.

#8 When looking up domestic violence information, remember to clear your browser. Most domestic violence websites have information about this on their site.

The primary thing to remember is that being with an abuser is not safe and should not be taken lightly. There are several resources available in your local area and on the internet that can be utilized to help you. I encourage you to visit your local library and search for resources that can help you. Please remember that most abusers will not let you go without a fight so by all means please be cautious and do not take his threats lightly.

WORDS
OF
FAITH

"I can do all things through Christ who strengthens me. I will not fear for God is always with me. When I am in trouble Christ will help me and make a way when there appears to be no way. I will divinely connect with people who will help me. I recognize that the angels of God will protect me from danger. Today, I will take steps towards getting out of this relationship. God has better plans for my life than to live like this and I believe that God's purpose for my life is greater than what is in front of me. My life is not over and I will get through this."

Psalm 46:1 (NIV)

God is our refuge and strength, an
ever-present help in trouble

Not Another Victim

CLOSING REMARKS

If I could walk every woman through the many transitions that come with a bad relationship, I would. But because I cannot my hope is that this book will help every reader become more aware of what is acceptable in a relationship.

Women have been fearfully and wonderfully made by God and should not tolerate a lazy, irresponsible or abusive man. Take the time to do some self evaluation and take charge of your life. Abuse should never be taken lightly. Some women year after year find themselves in another abusive relationship. Well that does not have to be you. You do not have to be another victim. These steps will help you renew your mind regarding the abuse. The main thing to realize is that God wants a better life for you. Lastly, please know that you deserve to live a life of peace and happiness. Today that peace and happiness can start. All you have to do is believe and take action.

God bless the readers of this book and may the peace of God fill your heart and your soul forever. Thank you for reading.

Not Another Victim

RESOURCES & HOTLINES

National Domestic Violence Hotline
1-800-799-7233
www.thehotline.org

National Dating Abuse Hotline
1-866-331-9474
www.loveisrespect.org

National Suicide Hotline
1-800-273-8255
www.suicidepreventionlifeline.org

Rape, Abuse and Incest National Network
1-800-656-4673
www.rainn.org

Not Another Victim

About the Author

Katha D. Blackwell is the first time author of *NOT ANOTHER VICTIM: A Woman's Guide to Avoiding a Bad Relationship.*

Born and raised in Chattanooga, Tennessee, Katha knew at a young age that she wanted to help people. After years of seeing women in her family go through many bad relationships, Katha decided to make it her goal to help women heal.

Katha attended college at Michigan State University and obtained a Bachelors in Political Science Pre-law. After graduating from Michigan State, she married her college sweetheart, Eric Blackwell. Katha obtained a Masters in Social Service Administration from The University of Chicago. Throughout Katha's college years, she provided individual and group counseling to abused women and children and also volunteered for various domestic violence programs.

In Katha's spare time, she enjoys nature walks, playing with her kids, watching movies, reading books and of course...writing. For more information or to send comments, please visit Katha's website at KathaBlackwell.com or email her directly at kathablackwell@yahoo.com

NOTES:

www.ingramcontent.com/pod-product-compliance
Lightning Source LLC
LaVergne TN
LVHW011223080426
835509LV00005B/294